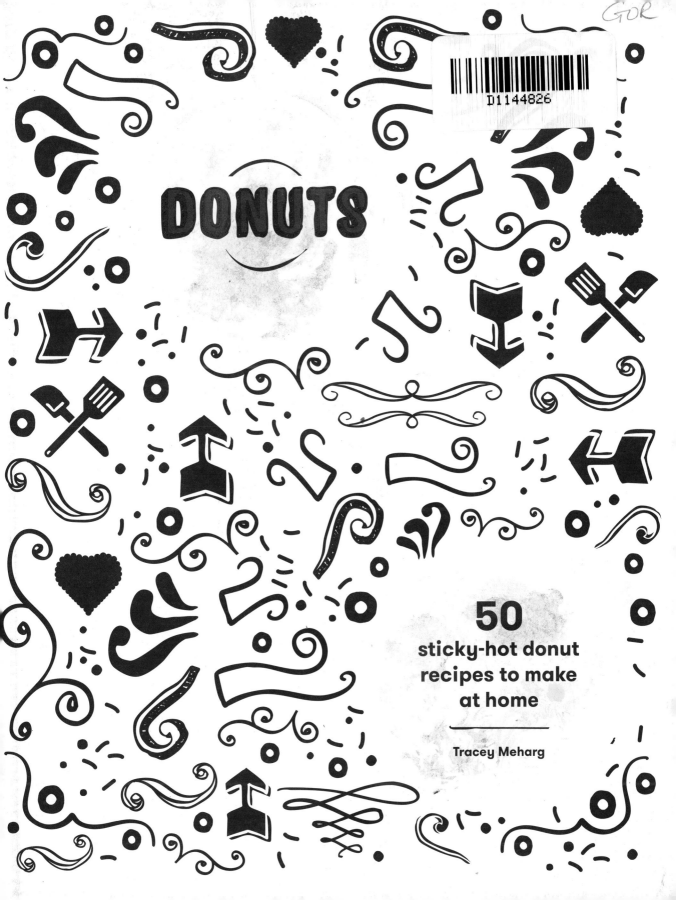

DONUTS

50
sticky-hot donut recipes to make at home

Tracey Meharg

DONUTS

50 sticky-hot donut recipes to make at home

Tracey Meharg

MURDOCH BOOKS

CONTENTS

The **donut** through **time**

Have you ever eaten a donut fresh out of the fryer or straight from the oven? If you have, you know how huge the gulf is between them and those stale off-the-shelf donuts, with their faux-cream, waxy frosting and claggy, squidgy fillings. Making your own is a commitment, but if you know how a good donut tastes, you'll know that these hot, scrumptious morsels are worth the effort. Recently, the real thing — the donut as it was meant to be — has been finding its way into more and more high-end restaurants and bakeries, with the food industry catching on that the donut, done right, can be truly sensational.

Donuts as we know them were brought over from the Netherlands to Manhattan in the early 1800s, when this area was still known as New Amsterdam. Called *olykoeks* or *oliebollen* — literally 'oil-cakes' or 'oil-balls' — they were filled with dried fruit and spices before being fried in oil, and are still a Christmas favourite in the Netherlands.

They were revolutionised in the 1840s when a ship-captain's mother, Elizabeth Gregory, cooked them for the crew — she put walnuts and hazelnuts in the middle (hence 'doughnuts'), perhaps to make them healthier, or perhaps to stop them being so greasy in the middle. Her son Hanson is credited with inventing the donut hole by cutting it out of the dough with a small tin, thereby transforming the donut into something that could be fried evenly all the way round. (Or, as another version of the story goes, he was at the ship's wheel when a storm hit, and he had to quickly impale the donut he was eating on a spoke so he could use both hands to steady the ship, accidentally making culinary history!)

After donut tin-cutters were patented in 1857, donuts fast became a staple in American homes, and by World War I they were so iconic that volunteers gave them out in the trenches in France to remind the soldiers of home. Soon after that came Joseph Levitt's infamous donut machine, which became a public spectacle in New York: the circle of dough dropping off into the vat of boiling oil, circulating, and then turning over, browning and emerging on a motorised ramp. It was a futuristic mystery, a sensation that had to be experienced first-hand.

But what is it about donuts that makes them so damn delicious? The secret is the temperature of the oil they are cooked in — by dropping them in very hot oil, the superheated steam puffs them up with air, making them literally light and fluffy. That, along with the hole, means the donut gets super hot, super fast: never doughy or dense.

The same goes for oven-baked donuts, which are just as delicious. They get hot fast, and that classic hole in the middle ensures they cook evenly, crisping up on the outside but staying fresh and steamy on the inside.

There are other iconic donuts across the world too, of course: the Israeli Hannukah specialty *sufganiyot* is now known worldwide as the godfather of the jam or jelly donut. There's also the slightly saltier, chocolate-dipped Mexican *churro*, which has its own mysterious origins: it may have been brought over by the Portuguese via China, or was possibly invented by Spanish shepherds as an alternative bread that could be cooked in the open air. Or from France, there's the *Pets de Nonne*, or nuns' fart, which is a crispy-tender dough often thickly dusted in powdered sugar. There's also more than a few Eastern takes on the donut, including the Indian *jalebi*, a celebration sweet which is a kind of pretzel-shaped donut, deep-fried and dipped in sugar syrup.

Now almost every country has their own homespun version, be they cream or custard-filled, topped with sweets for the kids or made with healthy options that combine the donut's perfect anatomy with whole foods and natural sugars.

Somewhere along the way, though, as it journeyed across the world, did the donut lose its zap? It made its way into hearts worldwide as a fast, delicious, tongue-burning treat, but has over the years become claggier, staler, neglected, made to sit on shelves for too long. But it doesn't have to be like that: it should be eaten fresh, and can be delectable fried or baked. It isn't doomed to die a death by preservatives and icing!

Donuts came from the home at Christmas-time, when it was coldest, and became so well-loved because they're heart-warming, decadent and comforting. Now they're re-entering gourmet menus, along with the introduction of the unlikely but undeniably fabulous croissant-donut. You don't need a deep-fryer to get these right, and they don't have to be greasy or doughy: they can be airy, fluffy and heavenly. So roll up your sleeves, and get them while they're hot!

CHAPTER 1

BASICS

YEAST DONUTS

These donuts have a lovely soft and chewy texture, making it hard to stop at just one. For the best results, be sure to enjoy these the same day you make them.

YEAST DONUTS

250 ml (9 fl oz/1 cup) lukewarm milk

3½ teaspoons dried yeast

450 g (1 lb/3 cups) plain (all-purpose) flour, plus extra for dusting

55 g (2 oz/¼ cup) caster (superfine) sugar

A good pinch of fine sea salt

1 egg, at room temperature, lightly whisked

30 g (1 oz) unsalted butter, melted, at room temperature

WHISK the milk and yeast together in a small, heatproof jug. Add 1 teaspoon of the flour and 1 teaspoon of the sugar, then whisk until well combined. Allow to stand at room temperature in a warm spot for 10–15 minutes, or until frothy.

PLACE the remaining flour, remaining sugar and the salt in the bowl of a standmixer. Attach the dough hook and mix together on a medium speed until well combined.

WITH the motor running, slowly add the egg, melted butter and the yeast mixture. Mix for 8 minutes, or until the dough is smooth and elastic (the dough should feel slightly sticky).

USING very lightly floured hands, scrape the dough into a lightly oiled bowl. Cover with a piece of baking paper, then a tea towel (dish towel). Set aside to rest in a warm, draught-free spot and leave for 1–1½ hours, or until the dough has doubled in size. (See pages 14–17, Tips for making yeast donuts.)

LINE two large baking trays with baking paper. Generously flour a work surface and gently tip the dough out onto it. Using a floured rolling pin, gently roll the dough out to a 1 cm (½ inch) thickness. Using a floured 8 cm (3¼ inch) round cookie cutter, cut out 10 rounds from the dough, making sure you cut them as close together as possible. Use a floured 3 cm (1¼ inch) round cookie cutter to cut out holes from the centre of each larger circle. Carefully transfer the donuts and their holes to the prepared trays, spreading them out in a single layer. Cover with tea towels then allow to rest for 40 minutes at room temperature, or until the donuts have doubled in size.

DEEP-FRY or bake and coat in cinnamon sugar as instructed on pages 30–31. Serve hot, warm or at room temperature.

Tips for making
yeast donuts

The dough needs to be left for 1–1½ hours to rise.

Use a floured rolling pin to gently roll out the dough.

Cut out rounds
from the dough,
making sure
you cut them as
close together
as possible.

Cut out holes from the centre of each larger circle.

CAKE DONUTS

These donuts are wonderfully quick to make — just like whipping up a cake batter — and are sure to be a hit with the kids too. Enjoy them on the day you make them, or store overnight in an airtight container at room temperature and reheat for a few seconds in the microwave until warm.

CAKE DONUTS

80 g (2¾ oz) unsalted butter, at room temperature

110 g (3¾ oz/½ cup) caster (superfine) sugar

1 egg, at room temperature

1 egg yolk, at room temperature

1 teaspoon vanilla essence

185 ml (6 fl oz/¾ cup) milk

500 g (1 lb 2 oz/3⅓ cups) self-raising flour, plus extra for dusting

A good pinch of fine sea salt

CREAM the butter and sugar together in a large standmixer for 3 minutes, or until pale and fluffy. Add the egg, egg yolk, vanilla essence and milk and mix until just combined.

SIFT the flour and salt over the mixture in the bowl. Mix until just combined, but do not overmix or the dough will become tough. (See pages 20–23, Tips for making cake donuts.)

LIGHTLY flour a work surface, turn the dough out onto it and, using lightly floured hands, gently bring together. Knead gently for a few seconds until the dough becomes smooth. Using a floured rolling pin, gently roll the dough out to a 1 cm (½ inch) thickness. Using a floured 8 cm (3¼ inch) round cookie cutter, cut out rounds from the dough, making sure you cut them as close together as possible. Re-roll any off-cuts and cut out more rounds until you have 12 in total. Use a floured 3 cm (1¼ inch) round cookie cutter to cut out holes from the centre of each larger circle.

DEEP-FRY or bake and coat in cinnamon sugar as instructed on pages 30–31. Serve hot, warm or at room temperature.

Tips for making
cake donuts

Mix the dough until just combined — do not overmix or the donuts will be tough.

Bring the dough together with your hands and knead gently.

Use a floured rolling pin to gently roll out the dough.

CROISSANT-DONUTS

A wonderfully decadent combination: croissant meets donut. A little patience and time is all that's needed to prepare these, and they are well worth the effort.

CROISSANT-DONUTS

185 ml (6 fl oz/¾ cup) lukewarm milk
3 teaspoons dried yeast
55 g (2 oz/¼ cup) caster (superfine) sugar
2 eggs, at room temperature, lightly whisked
1 teaspoon vanilla essence
450 g (1 lb/3 cups) plain (all-purpose) flour, plus extra for dusting
A good pinch of fine sea salt

BUTTER MIXTURE

35 g (1¼ oz/¼ cup) plain (all-purpose) flour
200 g (7 oz) unsalted butter, at room temperature

COMBINE the milk, yeast, sugar, eggs, vanilla essence, flour and salt in the bowl of a standmixer. Attach the dough hook then mix on a low speed until the ingredients are well combined. Increase the speed to medium–low and mix for 4 minutes, or until the dough is smooth and elastic (the dough will be sticky).

LINE a baking tray with baking paper that's been lightly floured, then transfer the dough. Using lightly floured fingertips, flatten the dough into a rectangle shape roughly 20 x 15 cm (8 x 6 inches). Cover with a piece of baking paper and refrigerate for 30 minutes.

BEAT the flour and butter for the butter mixture in a standmixer until smooth. Remove the chilled dough from the fridge and transfer it on the baking paper to a work surface. With a lightly floured rolling pin, roll out the dough to a 5 mm (¼ inch) thick rectangle roughly 30 x 20 cm (12 x 8 inches). Spread the butter mixture evenly over the dough, making sure you spread it right to the edges. (See pages 26–9, Tips for making croissant-donuts.)

FOLD the dough in thirds from the shorter sides, like a letter, then transfer back onto the tray on the baking paper. Cover with another sheet of baking paper and refrigerate for 30 minutes.

REMOVE the dough from the fridge and transfer to a clean piece of baking paper lightly dusted with flour. Turn the dough 90 degrees and roll it into the same-sized rectangle again, then fold both edges to the middle. Refrigerate for another 30 minutes, then repeat the whole turning, rolling, folding and chilling sequence twice more. Finally, turn, roll and fold the dough, then chill it for 1 hour.

LINE a large baking tray with baking paper. Lightly flour a work surface and a rolling pin and roll the chilled dough out to a 5 mm (¼ inch) thick rectangle roughly 30 x 20 cm (12 x 8 inches). Using a floured 8 cm (3¼ inch) round cookie cutter, cut out eight rounds from the dough, making sure you cut them as close together as possible. Use a floured 3 cm (1¼ inch) round cookie cutter to cut out holes from the centre of each larger circle. Carefully transfer the croissant-donuts and their holes to a prepared tray in a single layer. Cover with a tea towel (dish towel). Set aside to rest for 40 minutes at room temperature or until they have doubled in size.

DEEP-FRY and coat in cinnamon sugar as instructed on pages 30–31. Serve hot, warm or at room temperature.

Tips for making
croissant-donuts

Spread the butter
mixture evenly over the
rolled-out dough, right
to the edges.

Roll out the dough with a lightly floured rolling pin.

Fold the dough into thirds, like a letter.

How to **deep-fry**

When deep-frying donuts, make sure you use a saucepan that allows for a minimum depth of 5 cm (2 inches) for the oil. Only add the donuts to the oil when it has reached the desired temperature, otherwise they'll absorb too much oil and become stodgy, rather than being light and fluffy. To check this, you'll need a sugar thermometer, or you can drop a small amount of the donut off-cuts into the heated oil: it will immediately bubble around the edges if the oil is hot enough.

Vegetable, canola or rice bran oil, for deep-frying

HEAT the oil in a deep-fryer or a deep, heavy-based saucepan over a medium–high heat, or until the oil temperature reaches 180°C (350°F).

DEEP-FRY the donuts in batches, turning occasionally, for 2–3 minutes each, until puffed, golden and cooked through. Transfer to paper towel to drain before coating (see opposite) and serving.

DEEP-FRY the donut holes in three separate batches for 1–2 minutes each, or until puffed, golden and cooked through. Transfer to paper towel to drain before coating (see opposite) and serving.

How to **bake**

Baking donuts is a healthy alternative to deep-frying. You may find that some of the holes in the donuts close slightly on baking — if that happens, simply use the end of a wooden spoon to gently re-open the holes while the donuts are still hot.

100 g (3½ oz) unsalted butter, melted

PREHEAT the oven to 180°C (350°F/Gas 4). Line two large baking trays with baking paper. Place the donuts and donut holes 3 cm (1¼ inches) apart on the prepared trays.

BAKE the donuts, one tray at a time, for 10–12 minutes, or until puffed, light golden and cooked through (the donuts will sound hollow when their bases are tapped). Allow to cool for 3 minutes on the tray.

BRUSH lightly all over with the melted butter before coating (see below) and serving.

TO COAT
Everyone's favourite topping for donuts is cinnamon sugar. For 8–12 donuts, you'll need 220 g (7¾ oz/1 cup) sugar — white granulated sugar is best — and 2 teaspoons ground cinnamon. Combine in a deep, heatproof bowl, and have ready to toss the just-cooked donuts through!

Muesli donuts

Espresso cream-filled donuts

Lemon and poppy seed donuts

Maple syrup-glazed donuts
with crispy prosciutto

Blueberry donuts
with Earl Grey glaze

Peanut butter and
strawberry jam donuts

Banana donuts

Pretzel donuts

CHAPTER 2

WAKE UP AND SMELL THE DONUTS

MUESLI DONUTS

The perfect grab-and-go breakfast treat — all you need is a paper napkin.

CAKE DONUTS
80 g (2¾ oz) unsalted butter, at room temperature
110 g (3¾ oz/½ cup, firmly packed) light brown sugar
1 egg, at room temperature
1 egg yolk, at room temperature
2 teaspoons vanilla bean paste
185 ml (6 fl oz/¾ cup) milk
500 g (1 lb 2 oz/3⅓ cups) self-raising flour, plus extra for dusting
A good pinch of fine sea salt
Vegetable, canola or rice bran oil, for deep-frying

YOGHURT ICING
60 ml (2 fl oz/¼ cup) Greek-style vanilla bean yoghurt
185 g (6½ oz/1½ cups) icing (confectioners') sugar

TO SERVE
100 g (3½ oz/1 cup) store-bought toasted muesli (granola) with dried fruit

CREAM the butter and brown sugar together in a large standmixer for 3 minutes, or until pale and fluffy. Add the egg, egg yolk, vanilla bean paste and milk. Mix until just combined.

SIFT the flour and salt over the mixture in the bowl. Mix until just combined, but do not overmix or the dough will become tough.

LIGHTLY flour a clean surface, turn the dough out onto it and, using lightly floured hands, gently bring together. Knead gently for a few seconds until the dough becomes smooth. Using a floured rolling pin, gently roll the dough out to a 1 cm (½ inch) thickness. Using a floured 8 cm (3¼ inch) round cookie cutter, cut out rounds from the dough, making sure you cut them as close together as possible. Re-roll any off-cuts and cut out more rounds until you have 12 in total. Use a floured 3 cm (1¼ inch) round cookie cutter to cut out holes from the centre of each larger circle.

HEAT the oil in a deep, heavy-based saucepan over a medium–high heat until it reaches 180°C (350°F). Deep-fry the donuts in batches, turning occasionally, for 2–3 minutes each, or until puffed, golden and cooked through. Transfer to paper towels to drain, then allow to cool.

WHISK all of the ingredients for the yoghurt icing together in a bowl until well combined and smooth.

SPREAD the icing over the donuts then transfer to a wire rack set over a baking tray. Decorate the tops with toasted muesli and allow to set before serving.

ESPRESSO CREAM-FILLED DONUTS

These are guaranteed to boost a coffee-lover's energy levels in the morning!

YEAST DONUTS
250 ml (9 fl oz/1 cup) lukewarm milk
3½ teaspoons dried yeast
450 g (1 lb/3 cups) plain (all-purpose) flour, plus extra for dusting
55 g (2 oz/¼ cup) caster (superfine) sugar
A good pinch of fine sea salt
1 egg, at room temperature, lightly whisked
30 g (1 oz) unsalted butter, melted, at room temperature
Vegetable, canola or rice bran oil, for deep-frying

TO COAT
220 g (7¾ oz/1 cup) sugar
2 teaspoons ground cinnamon

ESPRESSO CREAM
300 ml (10½ fl oz) thickened (whipping) cream
2 tablespoons espresso coffee, cooled
110 g (3¾ oz/½ cup) caster (superfine) sugar

WHISK the milk and yeast together in a small, heatproof jug. Add 1 teaspoon of the flour and 1 teaspoon of the sugar and whisk until well combined. Allow to stand in a warm spot for 10–15 minutes, or until frothy.

PLACE the remaining flour, remaining sugar and the salt in the bowl of a standmixer. Attach the dough hook and mix together on a medium speed until well combined.

WITH the motor running, slowly add the egg, melted butter and the yeast mixture. Mix for 8 minutes, or until the dough is smooth and elastic (the dough should feel slightly sticky).

USING very lightly floured hands, scrape the dough into a lightly oiled bowl. Cover with a piece of baking paper then a tea towel (dish towel). Set aside to rest at room temperature in a warm, draught-free spot for 1–1½ hours, or until the dough has doubled in size.

LINE two large baking trays with baking paper. Generously flour a work surface and gently tip the dough out onto it. Using a floured rolling pin, gently roll the dough out to a 1 cm (½ inch) thickness. Using a floured 6 cm (2½ inch) round cookie cutter, cut out 18 rounds from the dough, making sure you cut them as close together as possible. Carefully transfer the donuts to the prepared trays, spreading them out in a single layer. Cover with tea towels and allow to rest for 40 minutes at room temperature, or until doubled in size.

COMBINE the sugar and cinnamon, for coating the donuts, in a deep, heatproof bowl.

HEAT the oil in a deep, heavy-based saucepan over a medium–high heat until it reaches 180°C (350°F). Deep-fry the donuts in batches, turning occasionally, for 2–3 minutes each, or until puffed, golden and cooked through. Transfer to paper towels to drain briefly and, while still hot, gently toss in the cinnamon sugar to coat on all sides. Allow to cool.

BEAT all the ingredients for the espresso cream together in a bowl until soft peaks form.

SPOON the mixture into a piping (icing) bag fitted with a 5 mm (¼ inch) round nozzle, then pipe into the centre of each donut and serve.

LEMON AND POPPY SEED DONUTS

Pretty and delicious, these are a lovely take on muffins.

CAKE DONUTS

80 g (2¾ oz) unsalted butter, at room temperature
110 g (3¾ oz/½ cup) caster (superfine) sugar
1 egg, at room temperature
1 egg yolk, at room temperature
1 teaspoon vanilla essence
185 ml (6 fl oz/¾ cup) milk
500 g (1 lb 2 oz/3⅓ cups) self-raising flour, plus extra for dusting
A good pinch of fine sea salt
1 tablespoon poppy seeds
2 tablespoons finely grated lemon zest
Vegetable, canola or rice bran oil, for deep-frying

TO COAT

220 g (7¾ oz/1 cup) sugar

LEMON BUTTERCREAM

60 g (2¼ oz) unsalted butter, at room temperature
250 g (8 oz/2 cups) icing (confectioners') sugar
2 tablespoons lemon juice

TO SERVE

1 teaspoon poppy seeds
Lemon zest strips

CREAM the butter and sugar together in a large standmixer for 3 minutes, or until pale and fluffy. Add the egg, egg yolk, vanilla essence and milk and mix until just combined.

SIFT the flour and salt over the mixture in the bowl. Add the poppy seeds and the lemon zest. Mix until just combined, but do not overmix or the dough will become tough.

LIGHTLY flour a clean surface, turn the dough out onto it and, using lightly floured hands, gently bring together. Knead gently for a few seconds until the dough becomes smooth. Using a floured rolling pin, gently roll the dough out to a 1 cm (½ inch) thickness. Using a floured 8 cm (3¼ inch) round cookie cutter, cut out rounds from the dough, making sure you cut them as close together as possible. Re-roll any off-cuts and cut out more rounds until you have 12 in total. Use a floured 3 cm (1¼ inch) round cookie cutter to cut out holes from the centre of each larger circle.

PLACE the sugar for coating in a deep, heatproof bowl.

HEAT the oil in a deep, heavy-based saucepan over a medium–high heat until it reaches 180°C (350°F). Deep-fry the donuts in batches, turning occasionally, for 2–3 minutes each, or until puffed, golden and cooked through. Transfer to paper towels to drain briefly and, while still hot, gently toss and roll in the sugar to coat on all sides. Allow to cool.

BEAT the butter for the buttercream for 3 minutes, or until very pale in colour and fluffy. Add the remaining ingredients and beat until well combined and smooth.

SPOON the buttercream into a piping (icing) bag fitted with a 1 cm (½ inch) star nozzle then pipe it over the centre of each donut. Sprinkle the tops with poppy seeds and lemon zest strips, then serve.

MAPLE SYRUP-GLAZED DONUTS WITH CRISPY PROSCIUTTO

The perfect balance of sweet and salty flavours, with the added crunch of crispy prosciutto.

YEAST DONUTS
250 ml (9 fl oz/1 cup) lukewarm milk
3½ teaspoons dried yeast
450 g (1 lb/3 cups) plain (all-purpose) flour, plus extra for dusting
55 g (2 oz/¼ cup) caster (superfine) sugar
A good pinch of fine sea salt
1 egg, at room temperature, lightly whisked
30 g (1 oz) unsalted butter, melted, at room temperature
Vegetable, canola or rice bran oil, for deep-frying

TO SERVE
4 thin slices prosciutto

MAPLE SYRUP GLAZE
125 g (4 oz/1 cup) icing (confectioners') sugar, sifted
80 ml (2½ fl oz/⅓ cup) maple syrup

WHISK the milk and yeast together in a small, heatproof jug. Add 1 teaspoon of the flour and 1 teaspoon of the sugar and whisk until well combined. Allow to stand in a warm spot for 10–15 minutes, or until frothy.

PLACE the remaining flour, remaining sugar and the salt in the bowl of a standmixer. Attach the dough hook and mix together on a medium speed until well combined.

WITH the motor running, slowly add the egg, melted butter and the yeast mixture. Mix for 8 minutes, or until the dough is smooth and elastic (the dough should feel slightly sticky).

USING very lightly floured hands, scrape the dough into a lightly oiled bowl. Cover with a piece of baking paper, then a tea towel (dish towel). Set aside to rest in a warm, draught-free spot for 1–1½ hours, or until the dough has doubled in size.

LINE two large baking trays with baking paper. Generously flour a work surface and gently tip the dough out onto it. Using a floured rolling pin, gently roll the dough out to a 1 cm (½ inch) thickness. Using a floured 8 cm (3¼ inch) round cookie cutter, cut out 10 rounds from the dough, making sure you cut them as close together as possible. Use a floured 3 cm (1¼ inch) round cookie cutter to cut out holes from the centre of each donut. Carefully transfer the donuts to the prepared trays, spreading them out in a single layer. Cover with tea towels. Rest for 40 minutes at room temperature or until doubled in size.

HEAT the oil in a deep, heavy-based saucepan over a medium–high heat until it reaches 180°C (350°F). Deep-fry the donuts in batches, turning occasionally, for 2–3 minutes each, or until puffed, golden and cooked through. Transfer to paper towels to drain briefly. Allow to cool.

MEANWHILE, cook the prosciutto on a foil-lined baking tray under a hot grill for 2–3 minutes, or until crisp and golden. Allow to cool, then break into small pieces.

WHISK the ingredients for the maple syrup glaze together in a bowl until well combined and smooth.

DIP the donuts, one at a time, into the glaze, then transfer to a wire rack set over a baking tray. Decorate the tops with prosciutto pieces and allow to set before serving.

BLUEBERRY DONUTS WITH EARL GREY GLAZE

The Earl Grey tea glaze on these donuts makes them a delicious addition to any morning tea.

CAKE DONUTS

80 g (2¾ oz) unsalted butter,
    at room temperature
110 g (3¾ oz/½ cup) caster
    (superfine) sugar
1 egg, at room temperature
1 egg yolk, at room temperature
70 g (2½ oz/½ cup)
    dried blueberries
1 teaspoon vanilla essence
185 ml (6 fl oz/¾ cup) milk
500 g (1 lb 2 oz/3⅓ cups)
    self-raising flour, plus extra
    for dusting
A good pinch of fine sea salt
Vegetable, canola or rice bran
    oil, for deep-frying
250 g (9 oz) blueberries

EARL GREY GLAZE

1 Earl Grey tea bag
60 ml (2 fl oz/¼ cup) boiling water
125 g (4½ oz/1 cup) icing
    (confectioners') sugar

CREAM the butter and sugar together in a large standmixer for 3 minutes, or until pale and fluffy. Add the egg, egg yolk, dried blueberries, vanilla essence and milk and mix until just combined.

SIFT the flour and salt over the mixture in the bowl. Mix until just combined, but do not overmix or the dough will become tough.

LIGHTLY flour a clean surface, turn the dough out onto it and, using lightly floured hands, gently bring together. Knead gently for a few seconds until the dough becomes smooth. Using a floured rolling pin, gently roll the dough out to a 1 cm (½ inch) thickness. Using a floured 8 cm (3¼ inch) round cookie cutter, cut out rounds from the dough, making sure you cut them as close together as possible. Re-roll any off-cuts and cut out more rounds until you have 12 in total. Use a floured 3 cm (1¼ inch) round cookie cutter to cut out holes from the centre of each larger circle.

HEAT the oil in a deep, heavy-based saucepan over a medium–high heat until it reaches 180°C (350°F). Deep-fry the donuts in batches, turning occasionally, for 2–3 minutes each, or until puffed, golden and cooked through. Transfer to paper towels to drain. Allow to cool.

TO make the glaze, steep the tea bag in the boiling water for 5 minutes. Remove and discard tea bag, then whisk the icing sugar and tea together in a bowl until well combined and smooth.

DIP the donuts, one at a time, in the glaze, then transfer to a wire rack set over a baking tray. Decorate the tops with fresh blueberries and allow to set before serving.

TIP YOU CAN ALSO DECORATE THE DONUTS WITH SMALL EDIBLE FLOWERS SUCH AS LAVENDER OR DRIED ROSE PETALS, IF YOU LIKE.

PEANUT BUTTER AND STRAWBERRY JAM DONUTS

Lock up your donuts! The kids will go crazy for these sweet 'n' salty treats.

CAKE DONUTS

50 g (1¾ oz) unsalted butter, at room temperature
140 g (5 oz/½ cup) crunchy peanut butter
110 g (3¾ oz/½ cup) caster (superfine) sugar
1 egg, at room temperature
1 egg yolk, at room temperature
½ teaspoon vanilla essence
185 ml (6 fl oz/¾ cup) milk
500 g (1 lb 2 oz/3⅓ cups) self-raising flour, plus extra for dusting
Vegetable, canola or rice bran oil, for deep-frying

TO COAT

220 g (7¾ oz/1 cup) sugar

TO SERVE

250 g (9 oz/¾ cup) strawberry jam, warmed
250 g (9 oz) small strawberries, thinly sliced

CREAM the butter, peanut butter and sugar together in a large standmixer for 3 minutes, or until pale and fluffy. Add the egg, egg yolk, vanilla essence and milk and mix until just combined.

SIFT the flour over the mixture in the bowl. Mix until just combined, but do not overmix or the dough will become tough.

LIGHTLY flour a clean surface, turn the dough out onto it and, using lightly floured hands, gently bring together. Knead gently for a few seconds until the dough becomes smooth. Using a floured rolling pin, gently roll the dough out to a 1 cm (½ inch) thickness. Using a floured 8 cm (3¼ inch) round cookie cutter, cut out rounds from the dough, making sure you cut them as close together as possible. Re-roll any off-cuts and cut out more rounds until you have 12 in total. Use a floured 3 cm (1¼ inch) round cookie cutter to cut out holes from the centre of each larger circle.

PLACE the sugar for coating in a deep, heatproof bowl.

HEAT the oil in a deep, heavy-based saucepan over a medium–high heat until it reaches 180°C (350°F). Deep-fry the donuts in batches, turning occasionally, for 2–3 minutes each, or until puffed, golden and cooked through. Transfer to paper towels to drain briefly, then gently roll the donuts in the sugar to coat the sides, and allow to cool.

SPOON the warm jam over the tops of the donuts and decorate with the strawberry slices. Allow to set before serving.

TIP YOU CAN ALSO DECORATE THE TOPS OF THE DONUT WITH CRUSHED, UNSALTED PEANUTS.

BANANA DONUTS

These heavenly donuts are baked, not fried, which means you can enjoy a few without feeling too guilty!

CAKE DONUTS

80 g (2¾ oz) unsalted butter,
    at room temperature
110 g (3¾ oz/½ cup, firmly
    packed) brown sugar
2 medium over-ripe bananas
1 egg, at room temperature
1 egg yolk, at room temperature
1 teaspoon vanilla essence
185 ml (6 fl oz/¾ cup) milk
550 g (1 lb 4 oz/3⅔ cups)
    self-raising flour
A good pinch of fine sea salt
¼ teaspoon ground cinnamon

CINNAMON GLAZE

125 g (4 oz/1 cup) icing
    (confectioners') sugar
½ teaspoon ground cinnamon
1½ tablespoons water

TO TOP

55 g (2 oz/½ cup) coarsely
    chopped walnuts, toasted
2 tablespoons coconut
    chips, toasted
2 tablespoons roughly crushed
    banana chips

CREAM the butter and sugar together in a large standmixer for 3 minutes, or until pale and fluffy. Add the bananas, egg, egg yolk, vanilla essence and milk and mix until just combined.

SIFT the flour, salt and cinnamon over the mixture in the bowl. Mix until just combined, but do not overmix or the dough will become tough.

LIGHTLY flour a clean surface, turn the dough out onto it and, using lightly floured hands, gently bring together. Knead gently for a few seconds until the dough becomes smooth. Using a floured rolling pin, gently roll the dough out to a 1 cm (½ inch) thickness. Using a floured 8 cm (3¼ inch) round cookie cutter, cut out rounds from the dough, making sure you cut them as close together as possible. Re-roll any off-cuts and cut out more rounds until you have 12 in total. Use a floured 3 cm (1¼ inch) round cookie cutter to cut out holes from the centre of each larger circle.

PREHEAT the oven to 180°C (350°F/Gas 4). Line two large baking trays with baking paper. Place the donuts about 3 cm (1¼ inches) apart on the prepared trays.

BAKE each tray of donuts for 12–15 minutes, or until puffed, light golden and cooked through (the donuts will sound hollow when the bases are tapped). Allow to cool on the trays for 3 minutes.

WHISK all of the cinnamon glaze ingredients together in a bowl until well combined and smooth.

DIP the donuts, one at a time, in the glaze, then transfer to a wire rack set over a baking tray. Sprinkle the tops with the walnuts, coconut chips and banana chips. Allow to set before serving.

PRETZEL DONUTS

These won't last long straight from the pan, and are perfect served alongside coffee.

YEAST DONUTS
250 ml (9 fl oz/1 cup) lukewarm milk
3½ teaspoons dried yeast
375 g (13 oz/2½ cups) plain (all-purpose) flour, plus extra for dusting
55 g (2 oz/¼ cup) caster (superfine) sugar
25 g (1 oz/½ cup) mini salted pretzels, crushed
A good pinch of fine sea salt
1 egg, at room temperature, lightly whisked
30 g (1 oz) unsalted butter, melted, at room temperature
Vegetable, canola or rice bran oil, for deep-frying

TO COAT
220 g (7¾ oz/1 cup) sugar
2 teaspoons ground cinnamon

WHISK the milk and yeast together in a small, heatproof jug. Add 1 teaspoon of the flour and 1 teaspoon of the sugar and whisk until well combined. Allow to stand at room temperature in a warm spot for 10–15 minutes, or until frothy.

PLACE the remaining flour, remaining sugar, the crushed pretzels and the salt in the bowl of a standmixer. Attach the dough hook and mix together on a medium speed until well combined.

WITH the motor running, slowly add the egg, melted butter and the yeast mixture. Mix for 8 minutes, or until the dough is smooth and elastic (the dough should feel slightly sticky).

USING very lightly floured hands, scrape the dough into a lightly oiled bowl. Cover with a piece of baking paper then a tea towel (dish towel). Set aside to rest at room temperature in a warm, draught-free spot for 1–1½ hours, or until the dough has doubled in size.

LINE two large baking trays with baking paper. Generously flour a work surface and gently tip the dough out onto it. Using a floured rolling pin, gently roll the dough out to a 1 cm (½ inch) thick rectangle about 30 x 28 cm (12 x 11¼ inches). Cut the rectangle in half lengthwise, then cut each half crosswise into eight wide strips. Twist each dough strip into a pretzel knot, then transfer the knots to the prepared trays and spread out in a single layer. Cover with tea towels and rest for 40 minutes at room temperature, or until doubled in size.

COMBINE the sugar and cinnamon, for coating the donuts, in a deep, heatproof bowl.

HEAT the oil in a deep, heavy-based saucepan over a medium–high heat until it reaches 180°C (350°F). Deep-fry the donuts in batches, turning occasionally, for 2–3 minutes each, or until puffed, golden and cooked through. Transfer to paper towels to drain briefly and, while still hot, gently roll in the cinnamon sugar to coat on all sides. Serve hot, warm or at room temperature.

Sherbet donut fruit kebabs

Donut shakers for boys and girls

Marshmallow chocolate donut whoopies

Cookies and cream donuts

Iced honey-cream donuts

Lamington donuts

Banana split donuts

Jelly star donuts

CHAPTER 3

FOR LITTLE KIDS
{AND BIG KIDS TOO}

SHERBET DONUT FRUIT KEBABS

A great healthy twist on a treat that the kids will have lots of fun eating.

CAKE DONUTS

80 g (2¾ oz) unsalted butter, at room temperature
110 g (3¾ oz/½ cup) caster (superfine) sugar
1 egg, at room temperature
1 egg yolk, at room temperature
1 teaspoon vanilla essence
185 ml (6 fl oz/¾ cup) milk
500 g (1 lb 2 oz/3⅓ cups) self-raising flour, plus extra for dusting
A good pinch of fine sea salt
Vegetable, canola or rice bran oil, for deep-frying

TO COAT

2 x 100 g (3½ oz) packets of powdered orange sherbet

TO SERVE

15 strawberries
4 kiwifruit, peeled, thickly sliced into rounds

CREAM the butter and sugar together in a large standmixer for 3 minutes, or until pale and fluffy. Add the egg, egg yolk, vanilla essence and milk, and mix until just combined.

SIFT the flour and salt over the mixture in the bowl. Mix until just combined, but do not overmix or the dough will become tough.

LIGHTLY flour a clean surface, turn the dough out onto it and, using lightly floured hands, gently bring together. Knead gently for a few seconds until the dough becomes smooth. Using a floured rolling pin, gently roll the dough out to a 1 cm (½ inch) thickness. Using a floured 4.5 cm (1¾ inch) round cookie cutter, cut out rounds from the dough, making sure you cut them as close together as possible. Re-roll any off-cuts and cut out more rounds until you have 30 in total.

HEAT the oil in a deep, heavy-based saucepan over a medium–high heat until it reaches 180°C (350°F). Deep-fry the donuts in batches, turning occasionally, for 2–3 minutes each, or until puffed, golden and cooked through. Transfer to paper towels to drain briefly, then allow to cool.

PUT the sherbet into a deep, heatproof bowl and gently toss and roll the donuts in the sherbet until coated on all sides. Using 15 wooden skewers, alternately thread two donuts, one strawberry and one slice of kiwifruit onto each one, then serve.

DONUT SHAKERS FOR BOYS AND GIRLS

These donuts add a little fun to the kitchen — great for parties and keeping little hands busy.

CAKE DONUTS
80 g (2¾ oz) unsalted butter,
    at room temperature
110 g (3¾ oz/½ cup) caster
    (superfine) sugar
1 egg, at room temperature
1 egg yolk, at room temperature
1 teaspoon vanilla essence
185 ml (6 fl oz/¾ cup) milk
500 g (1 lb 2 oz/3⅓ cups)
    self-raising flour, plus extra
    for dusting
A good pinch of fine sea salt

TO COAT
50 g (1¾ oz) unsalted butter
260 g (9¼ oz/¾ cup) honey

FAIRY DUST
140 g (5 oz) packet edible fairy
    glitter sprinkles
1 tablespoon small silver cachous

ZOO POO
45 g (1½ oz/⅓ cup) small
    chocolate balls
60 g (2 oz/⅓ cup) chocolate
    sprinkles

CREAM the butter and sugar together in a large standmixer for 3 minutes, or until pale and fluffy. Add the egg, egg yolk, vanilla essence and milk and mix until just combined.

SIFT the flour and salt over the mixture in the bowl. Mix until just combined, but do not overmix or the dough will become tough.

LIGHTLY flour a clean surface, turn the dough out onto it and, using lightly floured hands, gently bring together. Knead gently for a few seconds until the dough becomes smooth. Using a floured rolling pin, gently roll the dough out to a 1 cm (½ inch) thickness. Using a floured 3 cm (1¼ inch) round cookie cutter, cut out rounds from the dough, making sure you cut them as close together as possible. Re-roll any off-cuts and cut out more rounds until you have 80 in total.

PREHEAT the oven to 180°C (350°F/Gas 4). Line two large baking trays with baking paper. Place the donuts about 3 cm (1¼ inches) apart on the prepared trays.

BAKE each tray of donuts for 12–15 minutes, or until puffed, light golden and cooked through (the donuts will sound hollow when the bases are tapped). Allow to cool on the trays for 3 minutes.

MEANWHILE, place the butter and honey together in a small saucepan over a low heat, stir until the butter melts and the mixture is warm. Remove from the heat, transfer to a heatproof bowl and cover to keep warm.

COMBINE the ingredients for the fairy dust and zoo poo separately in different bowls. Divide the fairy dust between five paper bags and the zoo poo between another five paper bags.

WORKING in batches, quickly toss the warm donuts in the warm melted butter mixture to coat on all sides. Using tongs, divide the donuts evenly between the shaker bags. Hand to children and allow them to shake vigorously to coat on all sides. Serve warm.

MARSHMALLOW CHOCOLATE DONUT WHOOPIES

A seriously decadent treat. The homemade marshmallow adds a gooey yum factor.

CAKE DONUT WHOOPIES

80 g (2¾ oz) unsalted butter, at room temperature
110 g (3¾ oz/½ cup) caster (superfine) sugar
1 egg, at room temperature
1 egg yolk, at room temperature
1 teaspoon vanilla essence
185 ml (6 fl oz/¾ cup) milk
500 g (1 lb 2 oz/3⅓ cups) self-raising flour, plus extra for dusting
A good pinch of fine sea salt
55 g (2 oz/½ cup) cocoa powder

MARSHMALLOW

165 g (5¾ oz/¾ cup) sugar
125 ml (4 fl oz/½ cup) liquid glucose
2 egg whites, at room temperature
¼ teaspoon cream of tartar
2 teaspoons vanilla essence
12 drops red food colouring

TO SERVE

Icing (confectioners') sugar, for dusting

CREAM the butter and sugar together in a large standmixer for 3 minutes, or until pale and fluffy. Add the egg, egg yolk, vanilla essence and milk and mix until just combined.

SIFT the flour, salt and cocoa powder over the mixture in the bowl. Mix until just combined, but do not overmix or the dough will become tough.

LIGHTLY flour a clean surface, turn the dough out onto it and, using lightly floured hands, gently bring together. Knead gently for a few seconds until the dough becomes smooth. Using a floured rolling pin, gently roll the dough out to a 1 cm (½ inch) thickness. Using a floured 8 cm (3¼ inch) round cookie cutter, cut out rounds from the dough, making sure you cut them as close together as possible. Re-roll any off-cuts and cut out more rounds until you have 12 in total.

PREHEAT the oven to 180°C (350°F/Gas 4). Line two large baking trays with baking paper. Place the donuts about 3 cm (1¼ inches) apart on the prepared trays.

BAKE each tray of donuts for 12–15 minutes, or until puffed, light golden and cooked through (the donuts will sound hollow when the bases are tapped). Allow to cool completely on the trays. Halve the donuts by cutting horizontally through the centre.

STIR the sugar, glucose and 60 ml (2 fl oz/¼ cup) water for the marshmallow in a medium saucepan over a high heat until the sugar has dissolved. Bring to the boil, and boil for 8–10 minutes, or until the mixture reaches 130°C (250°F) on a sugar thermometer.

BEAT the egg whites and cream of tartar in a standmixer until soft peaks form then, with the motor running on a medium speed, slowly add the hot sugar mixture in a thin steady stream. Once added, increase the speed to medium–high and beat for 8 minutes, or until the mixture is stiff and glossy. Beat in the vanilla essence and red food colouring.

USING two dessertspoons, spoon the marshmallow mixture over the donut bases. Gently replace the donut tops, pushing down lightly (but do not allow the marshmallow to reach the edges because as it sets it will spread further). Leave the marshmallow to firm up, then lightly dust the tops with icing sugar and serve.

COOKIES AND CREAM DONUTS

These more-ish donuts will have the adults coming back for more, too.

YEAST DONUTS
250 ml (9 fl oz/1 cup)
    lukewarm milk
3½ teaspoons dried yeast
450 g (1 lb/3 cups) plain
    (all-purpose) flour, plus
    extra for dusting
55 g (2 oz/¼ cup) caster
    (superfine) sugar
A good pinch of fine sea salt
1 egg, at room temperature,
    lightly whisked
30 g (1 oz) unsalted butter,
    melted, at room temperature
Vegetable, canola or rice bran
    oil, for deep-frying

TO SERVE
80 g (2¾ oz/1 cup) mini
    cream-filled chocolate
    biscuits, roughly crushed

CHOCOLATE CREAM ICING
125 g (4½ oz/1 cup) icing
    (confectioners') sugar
30 g (1 oz/¼ cup) cocoa powder
80 ml (2½ fl oz/⅓ cup)
    thickened cream

COOKIE CREAM
500 ml (17 fl oz/2 cups) thickened
    (whipping) cream
120 g (4¼ oz/1½ cups) mini
    cream-filled chocolate biscuits,
    finely crushed

WHISK the milk and yeast together in a small, heatproof jug. Add 1 teaspoon of the flour and 1 teaspoon of the sugar and whisk until well combined. Leave to stand at room temperature in a warm spot for 10–15 minutes, or until frothy.

PLACE the remaining flour, remaining sugar and the salt in the bowl of a standmixer. Attach the dough hook and mix together on a medium speed until well combined.

WITH the motor running, slowly add the egg, melted butter and the yeast mixture. Mix for 8 minutes, or until the dough is smooth and elastic (the dough should feel slightly sticky).

USING very lightly floured hands, scrape the dough into a lightly oiled bowl. Cover with a piece of baking paper then a tea towel (dish towel). Set aside to rest at room temperature in a warm, draught-free spot for 1–1½ hours, or until the dough has doubled in size.

LINE two large baking trays with baking paper. Generously flour a work surface and gently tip the dough out onto it. Using a floured rolling pin, gently roll out to a 1 cm (½ inch) thickness. Using a floured 8 cm (3¼ inch) round cookie cutter, cut out 10 rounds from the dough, making sure you cut them as close together as possible. Use a floured 3 cm (1¼ inch) round cookie cutter to cut out holes from the centre of each larger circle. Transfer the donuts to the prepared trays in a single layer. Cover with tea towels. Rest for 40 minutes at room temperature or until doubled in size.

HEAT the oil in a deep, heavy-based saucepan over a medium–high heat until it reaches 180°C (350°F). Deep-fry the donuts in batches, turning occasionally, for 2–3 minutes each, or until puffed, golden and cooked through. Transfer to paper towels to drain briefly, then allow to cool.

WHISK all the ingredients for the chocolate cream icing together until well combined and smooth. Spread the icing over the tops of the donuts then transfer them to a wire rack set over a baking tray. Sprinkle with the roughly crushed biscuit and leave to set.

FOR the cookie cream, beat the cream until soft peaks form then fold through the crushed biscuit. Spoon into a piping (icing) bag fitted with a 1 cm (½ inch) star nozzle. Pipe the cookie cream into the donut centres, then serve.

ICED HONEY-CREAM DONUTS

Little boys and girls alike will love these cute, honey-flavoured treats.

YEAST DONUTS
250 ml (9 fl oz/1 cup) lukewarm milk
3½ teaspoons dried yeast
450 g (1 lb/3 cups) plain (all-purpose) flour, plus extra for dusting
55 g (2 oz/¼ cup) caster (superfine) sugar
A good pinch of fine sea salt
1 egg, at room temperature, lightly whisked
30 g (1 oz) unsalted butter, melted, at room temperature
Vegetable, canola or rice bran oil, for deep-frying

HONEY CREAM
300 ml (10½ fl oz) thickened (whipping) cream
2 tablespoons honey

ICING
125 g (4½ oz/1 cup) icing (confectioners') sugar
3 teaspoons milk
6 drops pink food colouring
4 drops blue food colouring

TO DECORATE
White buttons
Twine

WHISK the milk and yeast together in a small, heatproof jug. Add 1 teaspoon of the flour and 1 teaspoon of the sugar and whisk until well combined. Allow to stand at room temperature in a warm spot for 10–15 minutes, or until frothy.

PLACE the remaining flour, remaining sugar and the salt in the bowl of a standmixer. Attach the dough hook and mix together on a medium speed until well combined.

WITH the motor running, slowly add the egg, melted butter and the yeast mixture. Mix for 8 minutes, or until the dough is smooth and elastic (the dough should feel slightly sticky).

USING very lightly floured hands, scrape the dough into a lightly oiled bowl. Cover with a piece of baking paper, then a tea towel (dish towel). Set aside to rest at room temperature in a warm, draught-free spot for 1–1½ hours or until the dough has doubled in size.

LINE two large baking trays with baking paper. Generously flour a work surface, then tip the dough out onto it. Using a floured rolling pin, gently roll the dough out to a 1 cm (½ inch) thickness. Using a floured 6 cm (3¼ inch) round cookie cutter, cut out 18 rounds, cutting them as close together as possible. Carefully transfer the donuts to the prepared trays, spreading them out in single layers and cover with tea towels. Rest for 40 minutes at room temperature, or until doubled in size.

HEAT the oil in a deep, heavy-based saucepan over a medium–high heat until it reaches 180°C (350°F). Deep-fry the donuts in batches, turning occasionally, for 2–3 minutes each, or until puffed, golden and cooked through. Transfer to paper towels to drain, then allow to cool.

BEAT the honey cream ingredients together in a standmixer until soft peaks form. Spoon into a piping (icing) bag fitted with a 5 mm (¼ inch) round nozzle.

WHISK the icing ingredients together in a bowl until well combined and smooth. Halve the mixture and stir pink food colouring through one half and blue food colouring through the remaining half.

PIPE the honey cream into the centres of the donuts. Transfer to a wire rack set over a baking tray. Spoon either pink or blue icing over the donuts and allow to set. Thread the buttons onto lengths of twine and use these to tie stacks of the donuts together before serving.

LAMINGTON DONUTS

A modern twist on an Australian classic, these are the perfect size for popping into your mouth.

YEAST DONUTS

250 ml (9 fl oz/1 cup) lukewarm milk
3½ teaspoons dried yeast
450 g (1 lb/3 cups) plain (all-purpose) flour, plus extra for dusting
55 g (2 oz/¼ cup) caster (superfine) sugar
A good pinch of fine sea salt
1 egg, at room temperature, lightly whisked
30 g (1 oz) unsalted butter, melted, at room temperature
Vegetable, canola or rice bran oil, for deep-frying

LAMINGTON ICING

125 ml (4 fl oz/½ cup) boiling water
60 g (2¼ oz) unsalted butter
250 g (9 oz/2 cups) icing (confectioners') sugar
55 g (2 oz/½ cup) cocoa powder
270 g (9 oz/3 cups) desiccated coconut

WHISK the milk and yeast together in a small, heatproof jug. Add 1 teaspoon of the flour and 1 teaspoon of the sugar and whisk until well combined. Allow to stand at room temperature in a warm spot for 10–15 minutes, or until frothy.

PLACE the remaining flour, remaining sugar and the salt in the bowl of a standmixer. Attach the dough hook and mix together on a medium speed until well combined.

WITH the motor running, slowly add the egg, melted butter and the yeast mixture. Mix for 8 minutes, or until the dough is smooth and elastic (the dough should feel slightly sticky).

USING very lightly floured hands, scrape the dough into a lightly oiled bowl. Cover with a piece of baking paper then a tea towel (dish towel). Set aside to rest at room temperature in a warm, draught-free spot for 1–1½ hours, or until the dough has doubled in size.

LINE two large baking trays with baking paper. Generously flour a work surface and gently tip the dough out onto it. Using a floured rolling pin, gently roll the dough out to a 1 cm (½ inch) thickness. Using a floured 4.5 cm (1¾ inch) round cookie cutter, cut out 28 rounds from the dough, making sure you cut them as close together as possible. Carefully transfer the donuts to the prepared trays, spreading them out in a single layer. Cover with tea towels and rest for 40 minutes at room temperature, or until doubled in size.

HEAT the oil in a deep, heavy-based saucepan over a medium-high heat until it reaches 180°C (350°F). Deep-fry the donuts in batches, turning occasionally, for 2–3 minutes each, or until puffed, golden and cooked through. Transfer to paper towels to drain briefly, then allow to cool.

WHISK the water, butter, sugar and cocoa for the lamington icing together until well combined and smooth. Place the coconut in a bowl.

USING two forks, dip the donuts, one at a time, into the lamington icing to coat on all sides. Allow the excess to drip off, then gently roll in the coconut to coat. Transfer to a wire rack set over a baking tray and allow to set before serving.

BANANA SPLIT DONUTS

A great weekend sweet treat that the whole family will love.

YEAST DONUTS

250 ml (9 fl oz/1 cup) lukewarm milk
3½ teaspoons dried yeast
450 g (1 lb/3 cups) plain (all-purpose) flour, plus extra for dusting
55 g (2 oz/¼ cup) caster (superfine) sugar
A good pinch of fine sea salt
1 egg, at room temperature, lightly whisked
30 g (1 oz) unsalted butter, melted, at room temperature
Vegetable, canola or rice bran oil, for deep-frying

TO COAT

220 g (7¾ oz/1 cup) sugar
2 teaspoons ground cinnamon

TO SERVE

2 bananas, peeled, thinly sliced
45 g (1⅝ oz/⅓ cup) finely chopped unsalted roasted peanuts
10 red glace cherries

STRAWBERRY CREAM

300 ml (10½ fl oz) thickened (whipping) cream
165 g (5¾ oz/½ cup) strawberry jam

WHISK the milk and yeast together in a small, heatproof jug. Add 1 teaspoon of the flour and 1 teaspoon of the sugar and whisk until well combined. Allow to stand at room temperature in a warm spot for 10–15 minutes, or until frothy.

PLACE the remaining flour, remaining sugar and the salt in the bowl of a standmixer. Attach the dough hook and mix together on a medium speed until well combined.

WITH the motor running, slowly add the egg, melted butter and the yeast mixture. Mix for 8 minutes, or until the dough is smooth and elastic (the dough should feel slightly sticky).

USING very lightly floured hands, scrape the dough into a lightly oiled bowl. Cover with a piece of baking paper then a tea towel (dish towel). Set aside to rest at room temperature in a warm, draught-free spot for 1–1½ hours, or until the dough has doubled in size.

LINE two large baking trays with baking paper. Generously flour a work surface then gently tip the dough out onto it. Using a floured rolling pin, gently roll the dough out to a 1 cm (½ inch) thick rectangle about 25 x 15 cm (10 x 6 inches). Using a large floured knife, cut this rectangle in half lengthwise, then cut each piece into five wide strips crosswise to produce 10 smaller rectangles in total.

CAREFULLY transfer the square donuts to the prepared trays, placing them about 5 cm (2 inches) apart in a single layer. Cover with tea towels and rest for 40 minutes at room temperature, or until doubled in size.

COMBINE the sugar and cinnamon in a deep, heatproof bowl.

HEAT the oil in a deep, heavy-based saucepan over a medium–high heat until it reaches 180°C (350°F). Deep-fry the donuts in batches, turning occasionally, for 2–3 minutes each, or until puffed, golden and cooked through. Transfer to paper towels to drain briefly. While hot, roll in the cinnamon sugar to coat on all sides, then allow to cool.

FOR the strawberry cream, beat the cream until firm peaks form, then stir through the jam until well combined. Slice the cooled donuts through the top lengthwise, creating a pocket for the cream, being careful not to cut all the way through. Spoon the strawberry cream down the length of each donut, then top with banana, nuts and a glace cherry before serving.

JELLY STAR DONUTS

The jelly crystals add a sparkly touch to these donuts. You can use any flavour you like.

CAKE DONUT STARS
80 g (2¾ oz) unsalted butter, at room temperature
110 g (3¾ oz/½ cup) caster (superfine) sugar
1 egg, at room temperature
1 egg yolk, at room temperature
1 teaspoon vanilla essence
185 ml (6 fl oz/¾ cup) milk
500 g (1 lb 2 oz/3⅓ cups) self-raising flour, plus extra for dusting
A good pinch of fine sea salt
Vegetable, canola or rice bran oil, for deep-frying

TO COAT
1 x 85 g (3 oz) packet strawberry flavoured jelly crystals

CREAM the butter and sugar together in a large standmixer for 3 minutes, or until pale and fluffy. Add the egg, egg yolk, vanilla essence and milk and mix until just combined.

SIFT the flour and salt over the mixture in the bowl. Mix until just combined, but do not overmix or the dough will become tough.

LIGHTLY flour a clean surface, turn the dough out onto it and, using lightly floured hands, gently bring together. Knead gently for a few seconds until the dough becomes smooth. Using a floured rolling pin, gently roll the dough out to a 1 cm (½ inch) thickness. Using a floured 6 cm (2½ inch) star-shaped cookie cutter, cut out stars from the dough, making sure you cut them as close together as possible. Re-roll any off-cuts and cut out more stars until you have 28 in total.

PLACE the jelly crystals in a deep, heatproof bowl.

HEAT the oil in a deep, heavy-based saucepan over a medium–high heat until it reaches 180°C (350°F). Deep-fry the donuts in batches, turning occasionally, for 2–3 minutes each, or until puffed, golden and cooked through. Transfer to paper towels to drain briefly. While hot, toss the donuts in the jelly crystals to coat on all sides. Serve hot, warm or at room temperature.

Cosmopolitan-cocktail donuts

Lime cheesecake donuts

Apple crumble donuts

Éclair croissant-donuts

Strawberry brûlée croissant-donuts

Croissant-donut bites with
dulce de leche

Lemon meringue donuts

After-dinner choc-mint donuts

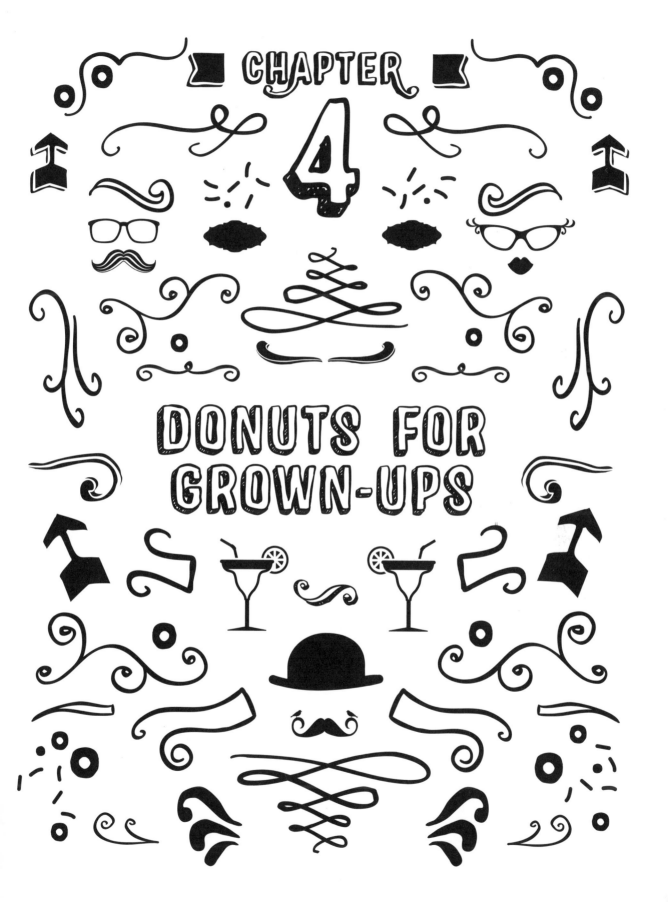

CHAPTER 4

DONUTS FOR GROWN-UPS

COSMOPOLITAN-COCKTAIL DONUTS

This adults-only donut has a boozy icing that's fit for any cocktail party.

CAKE DONUTS

80 g (2¾ oz) unsalted butter, at room temperature
55 g (½ cup) caster (superfine) sugar
1 egg, at room temperature
1 egg yolk, at room temperature
1 teaspoon vanilla essence
185 ml (6 fl oz/¾ cup) milk
500 g (1 lb 2 oz/3⅓ cups) self-raising flour, plus extra for dusting
A good pinch of fine sea salt
Vegetable, canola or rice bran oil, for deep-frying

COSMOPOLITAN ICING

125 g (4½ oz/1 cup) icing (confectioners') sugar
2 teaspoons citron vodka
½ teaspoon Cointreau
1½ tablespoons cranberry cordial

TO SERVE

Orange zest strips
Pink cachous

CREAM the butter and sugar together in a large standmixer for 3 minutes, or until pale and fluffy. Add the egg, egg yolk, vanilla essence and milk and mix until just combined.

SIFT the flour and salt over the mixture in the bowl. Mix until just combined, but do not overmix or the dough will become tough.

LIGHTLY flour a clean surface, turn the dough out onto it and, using lightly floured hands, gently bring together. Knead gently for a few seconds until the dough becomes smooth. Using a floured rolling pin, gently roll the dough out to a 1 cm (½ inch) thickness. Using a floured 8 cm (3¼ inch) round cookie cutter, cut out rounds from the dough, making sure you cut them as close together as possible. Re-roll any off-cuts and cut out more rounds until you have 12 in total. Use a floured 3 cm (1¼ inch) round cookie cutter to cut out holes from the centre of each larger circle.

HEAT the oil in a deep, heavy-based saucepan over a medium–high heat until it reaches 180°C (350°F). Deep-fry the donuts in batches, turning occasionally, for 2–3 minutes each, or until puffed, golden and cooked through. Transfer to paper towels to drain, then leave to cool.

MAKE the cosmopolitan icing by whisking all of the ingredients together in a bowl until well combined and smooth.

SPREAD the icing over each donut then transfer to a wire rack set over a baking tray. Decorate the tops with the orange zest and cachous. Allow to set and then serve.

LIME CHEESECAKE DONUTS

There is a wonderfully zingy taste of lime in this donut's cheesecake filling that makes for a great afternoon treat.

YEAST DONUTS

250 ml (9 fl oz/1 cup) lukewarm milk
3½ teaspoons dried yeast
450 g (1 lb/3 cups) plain (all-purpose) flour, plus extra for dusting
55 g (2 oz/¼ cup) caster (superfine) sugar
A good pinch of fine sea salt
1 egg, at room temperature, lightly whisked
30 g (1 oz) unsalted butter, melted, at room temperature
Vegetable, canola or rice bran oil, for deep-frying

TO COAT

220 g (7¾ oz/1 cup) sugar
1 tablespoon finely grated lime zest

LIME CHEESECAKE FILLING

125 g (4½ oz/½ cup) cream cheese
250 g (9 oz/1 cup) mascarpone cheese
2 tablespoons caster (superfine) sugar
2 teaspoons finely grated lime zest
80 ml (2½ fl oz/⅓ cup) freshly squeezed lime juice

WHISK the milk and yeast together in a small, heatproof jug. Add 1 teaspoon of the flour and 1 teaspoon of the sugar then whisk until well combined. Allow to stand at room temperature in a warm spot for 10–15 minutes, or until frothy.

PLACE the remaining flour, remaining sugar and the salt in the bowl of a standmixer. Attach the dough hook and mix together on a medium speed until well combined.

WITH the motor running, slowly add the egg, melted butter and the yeast mixture. Mix for 8 minutes, or until the dough is smooth and elastic (the dough should feel slightly sticky).

USING very lightly floured hands, scrape the dough into a lightly oiled bowl. Cover with a piece of baking paper, then a tea towel (dish towel). Set aside to rest at room temperature in a warm, draught-free spot for 1–1½ hours, or until the dough has doubled in size.

LINE two large baking trays with baking paper. Generously flour a work surface and gently tip the dough out onto it. Using a floured rolling pin, gently roll the dough out to a 1 cm (½ inch) thickness. Using a floured 6 cm (2½ inch) round cookie cutter, cut out 18 rounds from the dough, making sure you cut them as close together as possible. Carefully transfer the donuts to the prepared trays, spreading them out in a single layer. Cover with clean tea towels and leave to rest for 40 minutes at room temperature, or until they have doubled in size.

COMBINE the sugar and lime zest, for coating the donuts, in a deep, heatproof bowl.

HEAT the oil in a deep, heavy-based saucepan over a medium–high heat, or until it reaches 180°C (350°F). Deep-fry the donuts in batches, turning occasionally, for 2–3 minutes each, or until they are puffed, golden and cooked through. Transfer to paper towels to drain briefly then, while still hot, toss in the lime and sugar mixture to coat. Reserve any leftover lime sugar and leave the donuts to cool.

MAKE the lime cheesecake filling by beating the ingredients together in a bowl until well combined and smooth.

HALVE each donut horizontally through the centre then spoon the filling into the middle of each donut base. Replace the tops and push down firmly. Sprinkle with some of the leftover lime sugar before serving.

APPLE CRUMBLE DONUTS

Reminiscent of a classic winter dessert, these donuts have all the charm of tradition, but with a modern twist.

CRUMBLE TOPPING

50 g (1¾ oz) unsalted chilled
    butter, chopped
75 g (2½ oz/½ cup) plain
    (all-purpose) flour
55 g (2 oz/¼ cup, firmly packed)
    brown sugar
20 g (¾ oz/¼ cup) rolled oats
½ teaspoon ground mixed spice

CAKE DONUTS

80 g (2¾ oz) unsalted butter,
    at room temperature
55 g (2 oz/¼ cup) caster
    (superfine) sugar
60 ml (2 fl oz/¼ cup) apple purée
1 egg yolk, at room temperature
1 teaspoon vanilla essence
185 ml (6 fl oz/¾ cup) milk
500 g (1 lb 2 oz/3⅓ cups)
    self-raising flour, plus extra
    for dusting
A good pinch of fine sea salt
Vegetable, canola or rice bran
    oil, for deep-frying

APPLE GLAZE

125 g (4½ oz/1 cup) icing
    (confectioners') sugar
2 tablespoons apple juice

TO SERVE

2 large green apples
1 tablespoon lemon juice

PREHEAT the oven to 200°C (400°F/Gas 6). Line a baking tray with baking paper. Pulse the butter and flour for the crumble together in a food processor until coarse crumbs form. Transfer to a bowl, then stir through the remaining crumble ingredients. Spread out evenly on a baking tray lined with baking paper and bake for 10–12 minutes, or until crisp and golden. Allow to cool on the tray, then break into pieces.

CREAM the butter and sugar for the donuts together in a large standmixer for 3 minutes, or until pale and fluffy. Add the apple purée, egg yolk, vanilla essence and milk and mix until just combined.

SIFT the flour and salt over the mixture in the bowl. Mix until just combined, but do not overmix or the dough will become tough.

LIGHTLY flour a clean surface, turn the dough out onto it and, using lightly floured hands, gently bring together. Knead gently for a few seconds until the dough becomes smooth. Using a floured rolling pin, gently roll the dough out to a 1 cm (½ inch) thickness. Using a floured 8 cm (3¼ inch) round cookie cutter, cut out rounds from the dough, making sure you cut them as close together as possible. Re-roll any off-cuts and cut out more rounds until you have 12 in total. Use a floured 3 cm (1¼ inch) round cookie cutter to cut out holes from the centre of each larger circle.

HEAT the oil in a deep, heavy-based saucepan over a medium–high heat until it reaches 180°C (350°F). Deep-fry the donuts in batches for 2–3 minutes each, turning occasionally, or until cooked through, puffed and golden. Transfer to paper towels to drain then allow to cool.

WHISK the ingredients for the apple glaze together in a bowl until well combined and smooth.

DIP the donuts, one at a time, into the glaze. Transfer to a wire rack set over a baking tray and allow to set.

THINLY slice the apples and seed them, then quickly toss them in lemon juice to stop them from browning. Use them to top the donuts, then sprinkle with the crumble topping and serve.

ÉCLAIR CROISSANT-DONUTS

A lovely twist on a French pastry — yet even more delightful for their perfect little size.

CROISSANT-DONUTS

185 ml (6 fl oz/¾ cup) lukewarm milk

3 teaspoons dried yeast

55 g (2 oz/¼ cup) caster (superfine) sugar

2 eggs, at room temperature, lightly whisked

1 teaspoon vanilla essence

450 g (1 lb/3 cups) plain (all-purpose) flour, plus extra for dusting

A good pinch of fine sea salt

Vegetable, canola or rice bran oil, for deep-frying

BUTTER MIXTURE

35 g (1¼ oz/¼ cup) plain (all-purpose) flour

200 g (7 oz) unsalted butter, at room temperature

CHANTILLY CREAM

300 ml (10½ fl oz) thickened (whipping) cream

40 g (1½ oz/⅓ cup) icing (confectioners') sugar

2 teaspoons vanilla bean paste

TO SERVE

175 g (6 oz/1 cup) Belgian milk chocolate chips, melted

50 g (1¾ oz) raspberries, torn in half

icing (confectioners') sugar, for dusting

COMBINE the milk, yeast, sugar, eggs, vanilla essence, flour and salt in the bowl of a standmixer. Attach the dough hook and mix on a low speed until the ingredients are well combined. Increase the speed to medium–low and mix for 4 minutes, or until the dough is smooth and elastic (the dough will be sticky). Line a baking tray with baking paper and lightly flour it before transferring the dough onto the tray. Flatten to a rough 20 x 15 cm (8 x 6 inches) rectangle with lightly floured fingertips. Cover with another piece of baking paper and refrigerate for 30 minutes.

BEAT the flour and butter for the butter mixture in a standmixer until smooth. Transfer the chilled dough and paper to a work surface and roll out to a 5 mm (¼ inch) thick rectangle roughly 30 x 20 cm (12 x 8 inches). Spread the butter mixture evenly all over the dough, right to the edges. Fold the dough into thirds from the shorter sides, like a letter, then transfer back to the tray on the paper. Cover with baking paper and refrigerate for 30 minutes.

REMOVE the dough from the fridge, transfer to a clean piece of baking paper lightly dusted with flour, turn 90 degrees and roll into the same-sized rectangle again, then fold both edges to the middle. Refrigerate for 30 minutes, then repeat this turning, rolling, folding and chilling sequence twice more. Finally, turn, roll and fold the dough, then chill it for 1 hour.

LINE a large baking tray with baking paper. Lightly flour a work surface. Roll the chilled dough out to a 5 mm (¼ inch) thick rectangle roughly 30 x 20 cm (12 x 8 inches). Using a floured 6 cm (2½ inch) round cookie cutter, cut out 15 rounds from the dough, making sure you cut them as close together as possible. Carefully transfer to the prepared tray in a single layer. Cover with a tea towel (dish towel). Rest for 40 minutes at room temperature or until they have doubled in size.

HEAT the oil in a deep, heavy-based saucepan over medium–high heat until it reaches 180°C (350°F). Deep-fry the croissant-donuts in batches for 2–3 minutes each, turning occasionally, or until puffed, golden and cooked through. Transfer to paper towels to drain and allow to cool.

MAKE the chantilly cream by beating all of the ingredients together until soft peaks form. Spoon the mixture into a piping (icing) bag fitted with a 5 mm (¼ inch) round nozzle, then pipe the cream into the centre of each croissant-donut. Top with melted chocolate, then raspberries. Dust lightly with icing sugar and serve.

STRAWBERRY BRÛLÉE CROISSANT-DONUTS

These are perfect for a ladies' high tea. Make them during strawberry season for the best berry flavour.

CROISSANT-DONUTS

185 ml (6 fl oz/¾ cup) lukewarm milk
3 teaspoons dried yeast
55 g (2 oz/¼ cup) caster (superfine) sugar
2 eggs, at room temperature, lightly whisked
1 teaspoon vanilla essence
450 g (1 lb/3 cups) plain (all-purpose) flour, plus extra for dusting
A good pinch of fine sea salt
Vegetable, canola or rice bran oil, for deep-frying

BUTTER MIXTURE

35 g (1¼ oz/¼ cup) plain (all-purpose) flour
200 g (7 oz) unsalted butter, at room temperature

TO COAT

220 g (7¾ oz/1 cup) sugar
2 teaspoons ground cinnamon

TO SERVE

500 g (1 lb 2 oz) strawberries, halved
1 tablespoon caster (superfine) sugar

COMBINE the milk, yeast, sugar, eggs, vanilla, flour and salt in the bowl of a standmixer. Attach the dough hook and mix on a low speed until well combined. Increase the speed to medium–low and mix for 4 minutes or until the dough is smooth and elastic (the dough will be sticky).

LINE a baking tray with baking paper and lightly flour it before transferring the dough onto the tray. Flatten to a rough 20 x 15 cm (8 x 6 inches) rectangle with lightly floured fingertips. Cover with another piece of baking paper and refrigerate for 30 minutes.

BEAT the flour and butter in a standmixer until smooth. Roll the chilled dough out to a 5 mm (¼ inch) thick rectangle roughly 30 x 20 cm (12 x 8 inches). Spread the butter mixture evenly all over the dough, right to the edges. Fold the dough into thirds from the shorter sides, like a letter, then transfer back to the tray on the paper. Cover with baking paper and refrigerate for 30 minutes.

REMOVE the dough from the fridge, transfer to a clean piece of baking paper lightly dusted with flour, turn 90 degrees and roll it into the same-sized rectangle again, then fold both edges to the middle. Refrigerate for 30 minutes, then repeat this turning, rolling, folding and chilling sequence twice more. Finally, turn, roll and fold the dough, then chill it for 1 hour.

LINE a large baking tray with baking paper. Lightly flour a work surface. Roll the chilled dough out to a 5 mm (¼ inch) thick rectangle roughly 30 x 20 cm (12 x 8 inches). Using a floured 8 cm (3¼ inch) round cookie cutter, cut out eight rounds from the dough, making sure you cut them as close together as possible. Use a floured 3 cm (1¼ inch) round cookie cutter to cut out holes from the centre of each larger circle. Carefully transfer to the prepared tray in a single layer. Cover with a tea towel (dish towel) and rest for 40 minutes at room temperature or until doubled in size. Combine the sugar and cinnamon in a deep, heatproof bowl.

HEAT the oil in a deep, heavy-based saucepan over a medium–high heat until it reaches 180°C (350°F). Deep-fry the donuts in batches, turning occasionally, for 2–3 minutes each, or until puffed, golden and cooked through. Transfer to paper towels to drain then, while still hot, toss in the cinnamon sugar to coat.

PLACE the strawberries, cut-side up, on a foil-lined tray. Sprinkle with the sugar, then use a kitchen blowtorch to caramelise. Allow to cool, then serve with the croissant-donuts.

CROISSANT-DONUT BITES WITH DULCE DE LECHE

Decadence to the next level!
A platter of these deliciously
more-ish, sweet-and-salty
bites won't last long.

CROISSANT-DONUT BITES

185 ml (9 fl oz/¾ cup)
    lukewarm milk
3 teaspoons dried yeast
55 g (2 oz/¼ cup) caster
    (superfine) sugar
2 eggs, at room temperature,
    lightly whisked
1 teaspoon vanilla essence
450 g (1 lb/3 cups) plain
    (all-purpose) flour, plus extra
    for dusting
A good pinch of fine sea salt
Vegetable, canola or rice bran
    oil, for deep-frying

BUTTER MIXTURE

35 g (1¼ oz/¼ cup) plain
    (all-purpose) flour
200 g (7 oz) unsalted butter,
    at room temperature

TO SERVE

250 ml (9 fl oz/1 cup) dulce
    de leche
Pink sea salt flakes

COMBINE the milk, yeast, sugar, eggs, vanilla, flour and salt in the bowl of a standmixer. Attach the dough hook and mix on a low speed until well combined. Increase the speed to medium–low and mix for 4 minutes or until the dough is smooth and elastic (the dough will be sticky). Line a baking tray with baking paper and lightly flour it before transferring the dough onto the tray. Flatten to a rough 20 x 15 cm (8 x 6 inches) rectangle with lightly floured fingertips. Cover with another piece of baking paper and refrigerate for 30 minutes.

BEAT the flour and butter for the butter mixture in a standmixer until smooth. Transfer the chilled dough and paper to a work surface and roll out to a 5 mm (¼ inch) thick rectangle roughly 30 x 20 cm (12 x 8 inches). Spread the butter mixture evenly over the dough, right to the edges. Fold the dough in thirds from the shorter sides, like a letter, then transfer back to the tray on the paper. Cover with baking paper and refrigerate for 30 minutes.

REMOVE the dough from the fridge, transfer to a clean piece of baking paper lightly dusted with flour, turn 90 degrees and roll it into the same-sized rectangle again, then fold both edges to the middle. Refrigerate for 30 minutes, then repeat this turning, rolling, folding and chilling sequence twice more. Finally, turn, roll and fold the dough, then chill it for 1 hour.

LINE a large baking tray with baking paper. Lightly flour a work surface. Roll the chilled dough out to a 5 mm (¼ inch) thick rectangle roughly 30 x 20 cm (12 x 8 inches). Using a floured 3 cm (1¼ inch) round cookie cutter, cut out 44 rounds from the dough, making sure you cut them as close together as possible. Carefully transfer these bites to the prepared tray in a single layer. Cover with a tea towel (dish towel). Rest for 40 minutes at room temperature or until doubled in size.

HEAT the oil in a deep, heavy-based saucepan over a medium–high heat until it reaches 180°C (350°F). Deep-fry the bites in batches for 2–3 minutes each, turning occasionally, or until puffed, golden and cooked through. Transfer to paper towels to drain briefly.

PLACE the bites onto a serving platter and spoon the dulce de leche into a small serving bowl. Dip the bites into the dulce de leche to coat, sprinkle with pink sea salt and serve hot, warm or at room temperature.

LEMON MERINGUE DONUTS

With a touch of decorative meringue piping, these super-simple donuts are transformed into stunning works of art.

YEAST DONUTS
250 ml (9 fl oz/1 cup) lukewarm milk
3½ teaspoons dried yeast
450 g (1 lb/3 cups) plain (all-purpose) flour, plus extra for dusting
55 g (2 oz/¼ cup) caster (superfine) sugar
A good pinch of fine sea salt
1 egg, at room temperature, lightly whisked
30 g (1 oz) unsalted butter, melted, at room temperature
Vegetable, canola or rice bran oil, for deep-frying
320 g (11¼ oz/1 cup) lemon curd

MERINGUE
4 egg whites, at room temperature
150 g (5½ oz/⅔ cup) caster (superfine) sugar

TO SERVE
2 tablespoons finely grated lemon zest

WHISK the milk and yeast together in a small, heatproof jug. Add 1 teaspoon of the flour and 1 teaspoon of the sugar, then whisk until well combined. Allow to stand at room temperature in a warm spot for 10–15 minutes, or until frothy.

PLACE the remaining flour, the sugar and the salt in the bowl of a standmixer. Attach the dough hook and mix on a medium speed until well combined.

WITH the motor running, slowly add the egg, melted butter and the yeast mixture. Mix for 8 minutes, or until the dough is smooth and elastic (the dough should feel slightly sticky).

USING very lightly floured hands, scrape the dough into a lightly oiled bowl. Cover with a piece of baking paper, then a tea towel (dish towel). Set aside to rest at room temperature in a warm, draught-free spot for 1–1½ hours, or until the dough has doubled in size.

LINE two large baking trays with baking paper. Generously flour a work surface, then gently tip the dough out onto it. Using a floured rolling pin, gently roll the dough out to a 1 cm (½ inch) thickness. Using a floured 8 cm (3¼ inch) round cookie cutter, cut out 10 rounds from the dough, making sure you cut them as close together as possible. Use a floured 3 cm (1¼ inch) round cookie cutter to cut out holes from the centre of each larger circle. Carefully transfer the donuts to the prepared trays in a single layer, then cover with tea towels. Rest for 40 minutes at room temperature, or until doubled in size.

HEAT the oil in a deep, heavy-based saucepan over a medium–high heat until it reaches 180°C (350°F). Deep-fry the donuts in batches, turning occasionally, for 2–3 minutes each, or until puffed, golden and cooked through. Transfer to paper towels to drain. Allow to cool.

CUT the donuts in half horizontally and spread the bases with lemon curd. Replace the tops and transfer to the prepared trays.

MAKE the meringue by beating the egg whites in a standmixer until soft peaks form. Gradually beat in the sugar until firm peaks form and the sugar dissolves. Spoon the meringue into a piping (icing) bag fitted with a 1 cm (½ inch) star nozzle. Pipe the meringue over the tops of the donuts. Using a kitchen blowtorch, caramelise the meringue tops, then sprinkle with the lemon zest. Serve warm.

AFTER-DINNER CHOC-MINT DONUTS

Impress your dinner-party guests with these easy-to-prepare treats.

YEAST DONUTS

250 ml (9 fl oz/1 cup) lukewarm milk
3½ teaspoons dried yeast
450 g (1 lb/3 cups) plain (all-purpose) flour, plus extra for dusting
55 g (2 oz/¼ cup) caster (superfine) sugar
A good pinch of fine sea salt
1 egg, at room temperature, lightly whisked
30 g (1 oz) unsalted butter, melted, at room temperature
Vegetable, canola or rice bran oil, for deep-frying

CHOCOLATE ICING

125 g (4½ oz/1 cup) icing (confectioners') sugar
30 g (1 oz/¼ cup) cocoa powder
1–2 tablespoons boiling water

MINT DRIZZLE

60 g (2¼ oz/½ cup) icing (confectioners') sugar
1½ teaspoons peppermint essence
3 teaspoons boiling water

WHISK the milk and yeast together in a small, heatproof jug. Add 1 teaspoon of the flour and 1 teaspoon of the sugar, then whisk until well combined. Allow to stand at room temperature in a warm spot for 10–15 minutes, or until frothy.

PLACE the remaining flour, the sugar and the salt in the bowl of a standmixer. Attach the dough hook and mix together on medium speed until well combined.

WITH the motor running, slowly add the egg, melted butter and the yeast mixture. Mix for 8 minutes, or until the dough is smooth and elastic (the dough should feel slightly sticky).

USING very lightly floured hands, scrape the dough into a lightly oiled bowl. Cover with a piece of baking paper, then a tea towel (dish towel). Set aside to rest at room temperature in a warm, draught-free spot for 1–1½ hours, or until the dough has doubled in size.

LINE two large baking trays with baking paper. Generously flour a work surface then gently tip the dough out onto it. Using a floured rolling pin, gently roll the dough out to a 1 cm (½ inch) thickness. Using a floured 6 cm (2½ inch) round cookie cutter, cut out 18 rounds from the dough, making sure you cut them as close together as possible. Use the tip of a floured chopstick to push a hole through the centre of each donut. Carefully transfer the donuts to the prepared trays, spreading them out in a single layer. Cover with tea towels. Rest for 40 minutes at room temperature, or until doubled in size. Re-open the centre holes using a chopstick, if needed.

HEAT the oil in a deep, heavy-based saucepan over a medium–high heat until it reaches 180°C (350°F). Deep-fry the donuts in batches, turning occasionally, for 2–3 minutes each, or until puffed, golden and cooked through. Transfer to paper towels to drain, then allow to cool.

MAKE the icing by whisking all of the ingredients together in a bowl until well combined and smooth. Spread each donut with the chocolate icing, then transfer to a wire rack set over a baking tray. Allow to set.

WHISK all the ingredients for the mint drizzle together in a bowl until well combined and smooth. Spoon into a small re-sealable food storage bag. Snip one of the bottom corners off the bag and drizzle this mixture over the tops of the donuts. Allow to set, then serve.

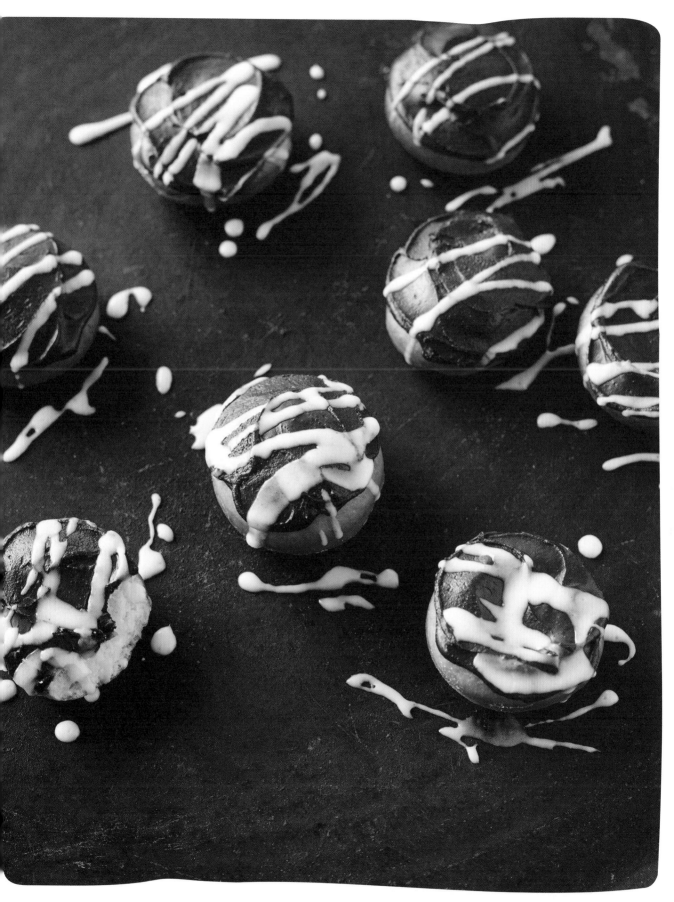

Sugar-free orange donuts

Supergreens donuts

Salted caramel vegan donuts

Coconut and date paleo donuts

Raw superfood donuts

Gluten-free mocha donuts

CHAPTER 5

ALMOST GOOD FOR YOU

SUGAR-FREE ORANGE DONUTS

These donuts contain rice malt syrup, which is made from fermented cooked rice and is much better for you than sugar, as it is fructose-free and full of slow-releasing energy.

YEAST DONUTS

125 ml (4 fl oz/½ cup) lukewarm water
3½ teaspoons dried yeast
450 g (1 lb/3 cups) plain (all-purpose) flour, plus extra for dusting
A good pinch of fine sea salt
1 egg, at room temperature, lightly whisked
30 g (1 oz) unsalted butter, melted, at room temperature
125 ml (4 fl oz/½ cup) freshly squeezed orange juice

ORANGE BUTTER

150 g (5½ oz) unsalted butter, at room temperature
60 ml (2 fl oz/¼ cup) rice malt syrup
1 tablespoon finely grated orange zest

TO SERVE

1 orange, peeled and segmented
Rice malt syrup, to drizzle

WHISK the water and yeast together in a small, heatproof jug. Add 1 teaspoon of the flour and whisk until well combined. Allow to stand at room temperature in a warm spot for 10–15 minutes, or until frothy.

PLACE the remaining flour and the salt in the bowl of a standmixer. Attach the dough hook and mix together on a medium speed until well combined.

WITH the motor running, slowly add the egg, butter, orange juice and then the yeast mixture. Mix for 8 minutes, or until the dough is smooth and elastic (the dough should feel slightly sticky).

USING very lightly floured hands, scrape the dough into a lightly oiled bowl. Cover with a piece of baking paper then a tea towel (dish towel). Set aside to rest at room temperature in a warm, draught-free spot for 1–1½ hours, or until the dough has doubled in size.

LINE two large baking trays with baking paper. Generously flour a work surface and gently tip the dough out onto it. Using a floured rolling pin, gently roll the dough out to a 1 cm (½ inch) thickness. Using a floured 8 cm (3¼ inch) round cookie cutter, cut out 10 rounds from the dough, making sure you cut them as close together as possible. Use a floured 3 cm (1¼ inch) round cookie cutter to cut out holes from the centre of each larger circle. Carefully transfer the donuts to the prepared trays, spreading them out in a single layer. Cover with tea towels, then leave to rest for 40 minutes at room temperature or until doubled in size.

PREHEAT the oven to 180°C (350°F/Gas 4). Line two large baking trays with baking paper. Place the donuts about 3 cm (1¼ inches) apart on the prepared trays.

BAKE each tray of donuts for 10–12 minutes, or until puffed, light golden and cooked through (the donuts will sound hollow when the bases are tapped). Allow to cool completely on the trays.

BEAT the butter for the orange butter for 3 minutes or until very pale and fluffy, then add the remaining ingredients and beat until well combined.

SPREAD the orange butter over the donuts and transfer to a wire rack set over a baking tray. Top each donut with an orange segment. Drizzle with rice malt syrup before serving.

SUPERGREENS DONUTS

Topping these donuts with some deliciously sweet kale chips not only makes them look gorgeous, but they'll taste great, too.

HONEYED KALE CHIPS
2 large kale leaves, stems removed and discarded, leaves torn into 3 cm (1¼ inch) pieces
2 tablespoons honey

CAKE DONUTS
80 g (2¾ oz) unsalted butter, at room temperature
110 g (3¾ oz/½ cup) caster (superfine) sugar
1 egg, at room temperature
1 egg yolk, at room temperature
1 teaspoon vanilla essence
185 ml (6 fl oz/¾ cup) milk
500 g (1 lb 2 oz/3⅓ cups) self-raising flour, plus extra for dusting
A good pinch of fine sea salt
2 teaspoons supergreens powder (see tip)

TO SERVE
Honey, to drizzle

PREHEAT the oven to 180°C (350°F/Gas 4). Line a large baking tray with baking paper and arrange the torn kale leaves on the tray. Drizzle the honey all over the leaves and bake for 8–10 minutes, or until the leaves are crisp and golden around the edges. Allow to cool on the tray.

MEANWHILE, cream the butter and sugar together in a standmixer for 3 minutes, or until pale and fluffy. Add the egg, egg yolk, vanilla essence and milk and mix until just combined.

SIFT the flour and salt over the mixture in the bowl. Add the supergreens powder and mix until just combined, but do not overmix or the dough will become tough. The supergreens powder will give the dough a marbled effect.

LIGHTLY flour a clean surface, turn the dough out onto it and, using lightly floured hands, gently bring it together. Knead gently for a few seconds until the dough becomes smooth. Using a floured rolling pin, gently roll the dough out to a 1 cm (½ inch) thickness. Using a floured 8 cm (3¼ inch) round cookie cutter, cut out rounds from the dough, making sure you cut them as close together as possible. Re-roll any off-cuts and cut out more rounds until you have 12 in total. Use a floured 3 cm (1¼ inch) round cookie cutter to cut out holes from the centre of each larger circle.

LINE two large baking trays with baking paper. Place the donuts 3 cm (1¼ inches) apart on the prepared trays.

BAKE each tray of donuts in the oven for 12–15 minutes, or until puffed, light golden and cooked through (the donuts will sound hollow when the bases are tapped). Cool for 3 minutes on the tray.

DRIZZLE the donuts generously with honey, then top with the honeyed kale chips. Serve hot, warm or at room temperature.

TIP SUPERGREENS POWDER IS AVAILABLE FROM HEALTH FOOD STORES AND SOME LARGER SUPERMARKETS.

SALTED CARAMEL VEGAN DONUTS

This salted caramel sugar topping gives these donuts a sweet–salty punch of flavour.

CAKE DONUTS

80 g (2¾ oz) dairy-free margarine spread, at room temperature
110 g (3¾ oz/½ cup) caster (superfine) sugar
45 g (1½ oz/⅓ cup) apple purée (see tip)
1 teaspoon vanilla essence
185 ml (6 fl oz/¾ cup) almond milk
500 g (1 lb 2 oz/3⅓ cups) self-raising flour, plus extra for dusting
A good pinch of fine sea salt

SALTED CARAMEL SUGAR

110 g (3¾ oz/½ cup) caster (superfine) sugar
110 g (3¾ oz/½ cup, firmly packed) dark brown sugar
2 teaspoons fine sea salt

CREAM the margarine spread and sugar together in a large standmixer for 3 minutes, or until pale and fluffy. Add the apple purée, vanilla essence and milk and mix until just combined.

SIFT the flour and salt over the mixture in the bowl. Mix until just combined, but do not overmix or the dough will become tough.

LIGHTLY flour a clean surface, turn the dough out onto it and, using lightly floured hands, gently bring it together. Knead gently for a few seconds until the dough becomes smooth. Using a floured rolling pin, gently roll the dough out to a 1 cm (½ inch) thickness. Using a floured 8 cm (3¼ inch) round cookie cutter, cut out rounds from the dough, making sure you cut them as close together as possible. Re-roll any off-cuts and cut out more rounds until you have 12 in total. Use a floured 3 cm (1¼ inch) round cookie cutter to cut out holes from the centre of each larger circle.

WHISK the ingredients for the salted caramel sugar together until well combined.

HEAT the oil in a deep, heavy-based saucepan over a medium–high heat until it reaches 180°C (350°F). Deep-fry the donuts in batches, turning occasionally, for 2–3 minutes each, or until puffed, golden and cooked through. Transfer to paper towels to drain briefly. While still hot, roll in the salted caramel sugar to coat on all sides. Serve hot, warm or at room temperature.

TIP APPLE PURÉE IS AVAILABLE IN SMALL TUBS IN THE CANNED FRUIT AISLE OF THE SUPERMARKET. IF USING APPLE SAUCE, YOU'LL ONLY NEED TO USE ¼ CUP AS IT IS A LOOSER CONSISTENCY.

COCONUT AND DATE PALEO DONUTS

These delicate donuts are grain-free and best served on the day of baking.

PALEO DONUTS

100 g (3½ oz) fresh dates
Boiling water, for soaking
60 ml (2 fl oz/¼ cup) coconut
    oil, softened
3 eggs, at room temperature
65 g (2¼ oz/½ cup) coconut flour
50 g (1¾ oz/½ cup) almond meal

TO SERVE

2 tablespoons maple syrup
20 g (¾ oz/¼ cup)
    desiccated coconut

PREHEAT the oven to 180°C (350°F/Gas 4). Grease 10 holes of a 12-hole non-stick donut tin.

SOAK the dates in boiling water for 15 minutes then drain. Remove their pits and pulse the flesh in a food processor until almost smooth.

STIR the coconut oil, eggs, coconut flour, almond meal, date mixture and 60 ml (2 fl oz/¼ cup) water together in a bowl until well combined and smooth. Spoon this mixture evenly into the prepared tin. Using your fingertips, press the mixture down firmly so you have a level surface. Bake for 15 minutes, or until the donuts are golden and firm when lightly pressed. Cool in the tin for 3 minutes then transfer to a wire rack set over a baking tray.

BRUSH the warm donuts generously with maple syrup and sprinkle with the desiccated coconut. Serve warm or at room temperature.

TIP PALEO REFERS TO FOODS THAT WERE AVAILABLE IN THE PALEOLITHIC (CAVEMAN) ERA: NOTHING PROCESSED, ONLY NATURAL INGREDIENTS.

RAW SUPERFOOD DONUTS

A super-rich chocolate treat — enjoy these straight from the fridge! Make a big batch as they keep well.

SUPERFOOD DONUTS

125 ml (4 fl oz/½ cup) coconut oil, melted
70 g (2½ oz/⅔ cup) raw cacao powder
2 tablespoons maca powder
125 ml (4 fl oz/½ cup) rice malt syrup
60 g (2¼ oz/⅓ cup) chia seeds
2 tablespoons LSA mix
2 tablespoons psyllium husks
2 tablespoons pepitas (pumpkin seeds)
2 tablespoons dried goji berries

TO COAT

Cacao nibs

GREASE a 12-hole non-stick donut tin.

STIR all the ingredients for the donuts together in a bowl until well combined.

SPOON this mixture evenly into the prepared tin. Using only your fingertips, press the mixture down firmly so you have a level surface.

COVER the tin with a tea towel (dish towel) and refrigerate for 30 minutes, or until the donut mix has almost set firm. Using a small palette knife, carefully remove the donuts from the tin. Roll them in cacao nibs, pressing down on the donuts for the nibs to adhere, until coated on all sides. Transfer the donuts to a baking tray lined with baking paper. Cover and chill for another hour, or until set firm. Serve chilled.

TIP THESE DONUTS WILL SOFTEN IF LEFT AT ROOM TEMPERATURE, SO SERVE THEM STRAIGHT FROM THE FRIDGE. THEY'LL KEEP IN AN AIRTIGHT CONTAINER IN THE FRIDGE FOR UP TO TWO WEEKS AND CAN ALSO BE KEPT IN THE FREEZER FOR UP TO ONE MONTH. SERVE AS A FROZEN TREAT ON HOT DAYS.

GLUTEN-FREE MOCHA DONUTS

These are perfect for a breakfast treat, or as a pick-me-up in the afternoon.

CAKE DONUTS

80 g (2¾ oz) unsalted butter,
   at room temperature
110 g (3¾ oz/½ cup) caster
   (superfine) sugar
1 egg, at room temperature
1 egg yolk, at room temperature
1 teaspoon vanilla essence
185 ml (6 fl oz/¾ cup) milk
500 g (1 lb 2 oz/3⅓ cups)
   gluten-free self-raising flour,
   plus extra for dusting
30 g (1 oz/¼ cup) cocoa powder
A good pinch of fine sea salt
1 tablespoon instant
   coffee granules
Vegetable, canola or rice bran
   oil, for deep-frying

MOCHA SUGAR

1½ teaspoons instant
   coffee granules
220 g (7¾ oz/1 cup) sugar
3 teaspoons cocoa powder

CREAM the butter and sugar together in a standmixer for 3 minutes, or until pale and fluffy. Add the egg, egg yolk, vanilla essence and milk and mix until just combined.

SIFT the flour, cocoa and salt over the mixture in the bowl. Add the coffee granules and mix until just combined, but do not overmix or the dough will become tough.

LIGHTLY flour a clean surface, turn the dough out onto it and, using lightly floured hands, gently bring together. Knead gently for a few seconds until the dough becomes smooth. Using a floured rolling pin, gently roll the dough out to a 1 cm (½ inch) thickness. Using a floured 8 cm (3¼ inch) round cookie cutter, cut out rounds from the dough, making sure you cut them as close together as possible. Re-roll any off-cuts and cut out more rounds until you have 12 in total. Use a floured 3 cm (1¼ inch) round cookie cutter to cut out holes from the centre of each larger circle.

USE a mortar and pestle to grind the coffee granules for the mocha sugar to a fine powder. Combine the coffee, sugar and cocoa powder in a deep, heatproof bowl.

HEAT the oil in a deep, heavy-based saucepan over a medium–high heat until it reaches 180°C (350°F). Deep-fry the donuts in batches, turning occasionally, for 2–3 minutes each, or until puffed, golden and cooked through. Transfer to paper towels to drain briefly then, while still hot, toss in the mocha sugar to coat on all sides. Serve hot, warm or at room temperature.

TIP AS ALL BRANDS OF GLUTEN-FREE SELF-RAISING FLOUR DIFFER IN TEXTURE, YOU MAY FIND THAT YOU NEED TO ADD A LITTLE MORE FLOUR OR A LITTLE MORE MILK TO GET THE DOUGH JUST RIGHT (THE CONSISTENCY SHOULD BE SOFT AND PLIABLE, NOT STICKY).

Sufganiyot (Israeli jam donuts)

Zeppole (Italian donuts)

Jalebi (Indian spiced donuts)

Loukoumades (Greek honey donuts)

Churros with chocolate dipping sauce

Sfenj (Moroccan donuts)

Pets de nonne (nuns' farts)

Oliebollen (Dutch fruit donuts)

Youtiao (Chinese donuts)

Persians (pink-iced Canadian donuts)

CHAPTER 6

AROUND THE WORLD

SUFGANIYOT ISRAELI JAM DONUTS

A delicious jam-filled donut eaten in Israel and enjoyed throughout the world during Hanukkah celebrations.

SUFGANIYOT
125 ml (4 fl oz/½ cup) lukewarm water
2 teaspoons dried yeast
450 g (1 lb/3 cups) plain (all-purpose) flour, plus extra for dusting
55 g (2 oz/¼ cup) caster (superfine) sugar
A good pinch of fine sea salt
1 teaspoon finely grated orange zest
2 egg yolks, at room temperature
1 egg, at room temperature
½ teaspoon vanilla essence
85 g (3 oz) unsalted butter, chopped
Vegetable, canola or rice bran oil, for deep-frying

TO SERVE
320 g (11¼ oz/1 cup) strawberry jam
Icing (confectioners') sugar, for dusting

WHISK the water and yeast together in a small, heatproof jug. Add 1 teaspoon of the flour and 1 teaspoon of the sugar and whisk until well combined. Allow to stand at room temperature in a warm spot for 10–15 minutes, or until frothy.

PLACE the remaining flour, remaining sugar and the salt in the bowl of a standmixer. Attach the dough hook and mix together on a medium speed until well combined.

WITH the motor running, slowly add the orange zest, egg yolks, egg, vanilla essence and then the yeast mixture. Mix for 4 minutes, or until well combined. Add the butter, a piece at a time, mixing for 4 minutes until the dough is smooth and elastic (it should feel slightly sticky).

USING very lightly floured hands, scrape the dough into a lightly oiled bowl. Cover with a piece of baking paper, then a tea towel (dish towel). Set aside to rest at room temperature in a warm, draught-free spot for 1–1½ hours, or until the dough has doubled in size.

LINE two large baking trays with baking paper. Generously flour a work surface and gently tip the dough out onto it. Using a floured rolling pin, gently roll the dough out to a 1 cm (½ inch) thickness. Using a floured 6 cm (2½ inch) round cookie cutter, cut out 18 rounds from the dough, making sure you cut them as close together as possible. Carefully transfer the sufganiyot to the prepared trays, spreading them out in a single layer. Cover with tea towels. Rest for 40 minutes at room temperature, or until doubled in size.

HEAT the oil in a deep, heavy-based saucepan over a medium–high heat until it reaches 180°C (350°F). Deep-fry the sufganiyot in batches, turning occasionally, for 2–3 minutes each, or until puffed, golden and cooked through. Transfer to paper towels to drain briefly, then allow to cool.

PULSE the jam in a food processor until smooth, then spoon it into a piping (icing) bag fitted with a 5 mm (¼ inch) round nozzle. Pipe the jam into the centres of the sufganiyot, then dust generously with icing sugar and serve.

ZEPPOLE  ITALIAN DONUTS

The dough of this southern Italian donut is enriched with fresh ricotta, making it beautifully soft and delicate.

ZEPPOLE

150 g (5½ oz/1 cup)
   self-raising flour
A good pinch of fine sea salt
1 tablespoon granulated sugar
230 g (8 oz/1 cup) ricotta cheese
2 eggs, at room temperature,
   lightly whisked
1 teaspoon vanilla essence
Vegetable, canola or rice bran
   oil, for deep-frying

TO SERVE

Icing (confectioners') sugar,
   for dusting

COMBINE the flour, salt, sugar, ricotta, eggs and vanilla essence in a bowl. Stir until the mixture is well combined (it should create a sticky batter).

HEAT the oil in a deep, heavy-based saucepan over a medium–high heat until it reaches 180°C (350°F). Using an oiled spoon, carefully drop tablespoons of the dough into the hot oil. Deep-fry the zeppole in batches, turning occasionally, for 2–3 minutes each, or until they are puffed, golden and cooked through.

TRANSFER to paper towels to drain briefly. Dust generously with icing sugar and serve warm.

JALEBI INDIAN SPICED DONUTS

These super-sweet Indian treats are submerged in saffron syrup, which gives them a beautifully pale orange colour.

JALEBI

150 g (5½ oz/1 cup) plain
    (all-purpose) flour
140 g (5 oz/½ cup) plain yoghurt
A good pinch of bicarbonate
    of soda (baking soda)
Ghee (clarified butter), vegetable,
    canola or rice bran oil, for
    deep-frying

SAFFRON SYRUP

220 g (7¾ oz/1 cup) sugar
½ teaspoon saffron threads

WHISK the flour, yoghurt and 185 ml (6 fl oz/¾ cup) water together in a bowl until well combined and smooth. Whisk in the bicarbonate of soda until well combined.

SPOON the batter into a piping (icing) bag fitted with a 5 mm (¼ inch) round nozzle, then place in the refrigerator and chill until required.

PLACE the sugar and 125 ml (4 fl oz/½ cup) water for the saffron syrup in a small saucepan over a high heat. Stir gently until the sugar dissolves, then bring to the boil for 2 minutes, or until slightly reduced. Remove the pan from the heat, stir in the saffron threads, then cover to keep warm.

WHEN ready to cook, heat the ghee or oil in a deep, heavy-based saucepan over a medium–high heat until it reaches 180°C (350°F). Carefully pipe the chilled batter into the hot oil, forming concentric circles so each jalebi is about 8 cm (3¼ inches) wide. Deep-fry the jalebi in batches, turning occasionally, for 2–3 minutes each, or until lightly puffed, golden and cooked through.

TRANSFER to paper towels to drain briefly, then submerge the hot jalebi in the warm saffron syrup. Using a slotted spoon, remove them from the syrup and allow any excess to drain away. Transfer to a serving platter and serve warm.

 GREEK HONEY DONUTS

These syrup-drenched Greek donuts are served warm, lightly dusted with cinnamon.

LOUKOUMADES

60 ml (2 fl oz/¼ cup)
    lukewarm water, plus 185 ml
    (6 fl oz/¾ cup) extra
1 teaspoon dried yeast
2 teaspoons caster
    (superfine) sugar
260 g (9¼ oz/1¾ cups) plain
    (all-purpose) flour
A good pinch of fine sea salt
½ teaspoon vanilla essence
Vegetable, canola or rice bran
    oil, for deep-frying

HONEY SYRUP

125 g (4½ oz/⅓ cup) honey

TO SERVE

Ground cinnamon, for dusting

WHISK the 60 ml of water and yeast together in a large bowl. Add the sugar and 1 teaspoon of the flour and whisk until well combined. Allow to stand at room temperature in a warm spot for 10–15 minutes, or until frothy.

ADD the remaining flour, the salt, vanilla essence and the extra 185 ml of water to the yeast mixture. Stir until well combined and smooth. Cover the bowl with a piece of baking paper, then a tea towel (dish towel) and set aside to rest in a warm, draught-free spot for 1–1½ hours, or until the dough has doubled in size.

PLACE the honey for the honey syrup in a small saucepan over a high heat with 125 ml (4 fl oz/½ cup) of water. Bring to the boil, then remove the pan from the heat and allow the syrup to cool in the pan.

LINE two large baking trays with baking paper.

HEAT the oil in a deep, heavy-based saucepan over a medium–high heat until it reaches 180°C (350°F). Using an oiled dessertspoon, carefully drop spoonfuls of the batter into the hot oil. Deep-fry in batches, turning occasionally, for 2–3 minutes each, or until the loukoumades are puffed, golden and cooked through. Drain briefly on paper towels, then transfer to the prepared trays.

DRIZZLE with the honey syrup, dust with cinnamon and serve warm.

CHURROS WITH CHOCOLATE DIPPING SAUCE

These Spanish donuts are irresistible when served warm with this decadent chocolate dipping sauce. Delicious in the morning with coffee, or in the evening as a luxurious dessert.

CHURROS
100 g (3½ oz) unsalted butter, chopped
150 g (5½ oz/1 cup) plain (all-purpose) flour
¼ teaspoon salt
2 eggs, at room temperature
Vegetable, canola or rice bran oil, for deep-frying

TO COAT
220 g (7¾ oz/1 cup) sugar
2 teaspoons ground cinnamon

CHOCOLATE DIPPING SAUCE
200 g (7 oz) good-quality dark chocolate, coarsely chopped
300 ml (10½ fl oz) thin (pouring) cream

PLACE the butter and 250 ml (9 fl oz/1 cup) of water together in a medium saucepan over a high heat. Bring to the boil, stirring until the butter melts. Add the flour and salt and stir vigorously for 1 minute, or until the mixture comes together in a ball. Remove from the heat.

TRANSFER the flour mixture to the bowl of a standmixer. Allow to stand for 10 minutes to cool slightly, then attach the paddle and beat on a medium speed for 3 minutes. Add the eggs, one at a time, beating well between each addition until the mixture is combined and glossy.

SPOON the dough into a piping (icing) bag fitted with a 1 cm (½ inch) star nozzle.

COMBINE the sugar and cinnamon, for coating the churros, in a deep, heatproof bowl.

PLACE the chopped chocolate and cream for the chocolate sauce in a heatproof bowl set over a saucepan of simmering water. Make sure the base of the bowl is not touching the water in the pan. Stir gently until the mixture melts together and is smooth. Remove the pan from the heat and set aside (keep the bowl set over the pan so the sauce stays warm).

HEAT the oil in a deep, heavy-based saucepan over a medium–high heat until it reaches 180°C (350°F). Carefully pipe 8 cm (3¼ inch) lengths of dough into the hot oil. Deep-fry in batches, turning occasionally, for 2–3 minutes each, or until the churros are puffed, golden and cooked through. Transfer to paper towels to drain briefly then, while still hot, toss the churros in the cinnamon sugar to coat on all sides. Serve warm with the warm chocolate dipping sauce.

SFENJ MOROCCAN DONUTS

These donuts are made from unsweetened dough, and once cooked, can be rolled in sugar or icing sugar.

SFENJ
250 ml (9 fl oz/1 cup) lukewarm water
1 tablespoon dried yeast
2 tablespoons sugar
450 g (1 lb/3 cups) plain (all-purpose) flour, plus extra for dusting
A good pinch of fine sea salt

TO COAT
220 g (7¾ oz/1 cup) sugar

WHISK the water and yeast together in the bowl of a standmixer. Add the sugar and 1 teaspoon of the flour, then whisk until well combined. Allow to stand in a warm spot for 10–15 minutes, or until frothy.

ADD the remaining flour and the salt to the yeast mixture. Attach the dough hook and mix on a medium speed until well combined, then mix for 8 minutes more, or until the dough is smooth and elastic (the dough will feel firm).

GENEROUSLY oil a large bowl. Add the dough and turn to coat (it needs to be coated on all sides as this will prevent a crust from forming on the dough). Cover with plastic wrap, then a tea towel (dish towel) and set aside to rest in a warm, draught-free spot for 1–1½ hours, or until the dough has doubled in size. Press the dough down with the palms of your hands to expel some of the air.

HEAT the oil in a deep, heavy-based saucepan over a medium–high heat until it reaches 180°C (350°F).

LIGHTLY dust a clean surface with flour then divide the dough into 12 equal portions. Knead each portion until smooth, flatten into 6 cm (2½ inch) rounds in your palms, then push a finger through the centre to create a hole. Twirl the dough on your finger to enlarge the hole to the size of a tennis ball.

PLACE the sugar for coating in a deep, heatproof bowl.

DEEP-FRY the sfenj in batches, turning occasionally, for 2–3 minutes each, or until they are puffed, golden and cooked through. Transfer to paper towels to drain briefly then, while still hot, toss in sugar to coat on all sides. Serve warm.

PETS DE NONNE NUNS' FARTS

These little French donuts are surprisingly light and airy, which gives them their cheeky name.

PETS DE NONNE
60 g (2¼ oz) unsalted
    butter, chopped
A good pinch of fine sea salt
75 g (2¾ oz/½ cup) plain
    (all-purpose) flour
2 eggs, at room temperature
Vegetable, canola or rice bran
    oil, for deep-frying

TO SERVE
Icing (confectioners') sugar,
    for dusting

PLACE the butter and 125 ml (4 fl oz/½ cup) water in a saucepan over a high heat. Bring to the boil, stirring until the butter melts. Add the salt and flour and stir vigorously for 1 minute, or until the mixture comes together in a ball. Remove from the heat.

TRANSFER the flour mixture to the bowl of a standmixer. Allow to stand for 10 minutes to cool slightly, then attach the paddle and beat on a medium speed for 3 minutes. Add the eggs, one at a time, beating well between each addition until the mixture is well combined and glossy (it should be soft and sticky).

HEAT the oil in a deep, heavy-based saucepan over a medium–high heat until it reaches 180°C (350°F). Using an oiled teaspoon, carefully drop heaped teaspoons of the dough into the hot oil. Deep-fry the *pets de nonne* in batches, turning occasionally, for 2–3 minutes each, or until puffed, golden and cooked through. Transfer to paper towels to drain, then allow to cool. Dust generously with icing sugar before serving.

OLIEBOLLEN DUTCH FRUIT DONUTS

Traditionally eaten by the Dutch on New Year's Eve (and enjoyed in Belgium, too), these fruit-filled delicacies are affectionately known as 'dutchies' elsewhere in the world.

OLIEBOLLEN

60 ml (2 fl oz/¼ cup) lukewarm water
2 teaspoons dried yeast
2 tablespoons sugar
225 g (8 oz/1½ cups) plain (all-purpose) flour
A good pinch of fine sea salt
125 ml (4 fl oz/½ cup) milk
1 egg, at room temperature, lightly whisked
40 g (1½ oz/¼ cup) currants
50 g (1¾ oz/⅓ cup) raisins
1 small green apple, peeled, cored, finely chopped
Vegetable, canola or rice bran oil, for deep-frying

TO SERVE

Icing (confectioners') sugar, for dusting

WHISK the water and yeast together in a large bowl. Add the sugar and whisk until well combined. Allow to stand in a warm spot for 10–15 minutes, or until frothy.

ADD the flour, salt, milk, egg, currants, raisins and apple to the yeast mixture. Stir until well combined, then cover with a piece of baking paper and a tea towel (dish towel). Set aside to rest in a warm, draught-free spot for 1–1½ hours, or until the dough has doubled in size (the mixture will be soft and sticky).

HEAT the oil in a deep, heavy-based saucepan over a medium–high heat until it reaches 180°C (350°F). Using an oiled dessertspoon, carefully drop spoonfuls of the dough into the hot oil. Deep-fry the oliebollen in batches, turning occasionally, for 2–3 minutes each, or until puffed, golden and cooked through.

TRANSFER to paper towels to drain briefly. Dust generously with icing sugar and serve warm.

YOUTIAO CHINESE DONUTS

Also known as Chinese oil sticks, these are eaten piping hot and crispy alongside savoury rice dishes, or used for dipping into hot coffee or chocolate.

YOUTIAO

500 g (1 lb 2 oz/3⅓ cups) plain (all-purpose) flour, plus extra for dusting
1 teaspoon dried yeast
1 teaspoon baking powder
1 teaspoon fine sea salt
2 tablespoons sugar
375 ml (13 fl oz/1½ cups) lukewarm water
Vegetable, canola or rice bran oil, for deep-frying

PLACE all of the ingredients for the youtiao in the bowl of a standmixer. Attach the dough hook and mix together on a medium speed until well combined, then mix for 5 minutes more, or until the dough is smooth and elastic (the dough will feel slightly sticky).

TRANSFER the dough to a lightly oiled bowl, cover with a piece of baking paper, then a tea towel (dish towel). Set aside to rest in a warm, draught-free spot for 1–1½ hours, or until the dough has doubled in size.

LINE two large baking trays with baking paper. Generously flour a work surface and gently tip the dough out onto it. Using a floured rolling pin, roll the dough out to a 5 mm (¼ inch) thick, 40 x 20 cm (16 x 8 inches) rectangle. Using a large floured knife, cut the dough into 2 cm (¾ inch) wide strips crosswise until you have 40 strips. Wet a finger in a bowl of water, then run it down the length of a strip and place another strip on top, pressing down lightly to seal them together. Transfer to a prepared tray, then repeat until you have used up the rest of the dough. Allow to rest for 15 minutes at room temperature, or until the sticks are slightly puffed up.

HEAT the oil in a deep, heavy-based frying pan over a medium–high heat until it reaches 180°C (350°F). Deep-fry the youtiao in batches, turning occasionally, for 2–3 minutes each, or until puffed, golden and cooked through.

TRANSFER to paper towels to drain briefly, then serve hot.

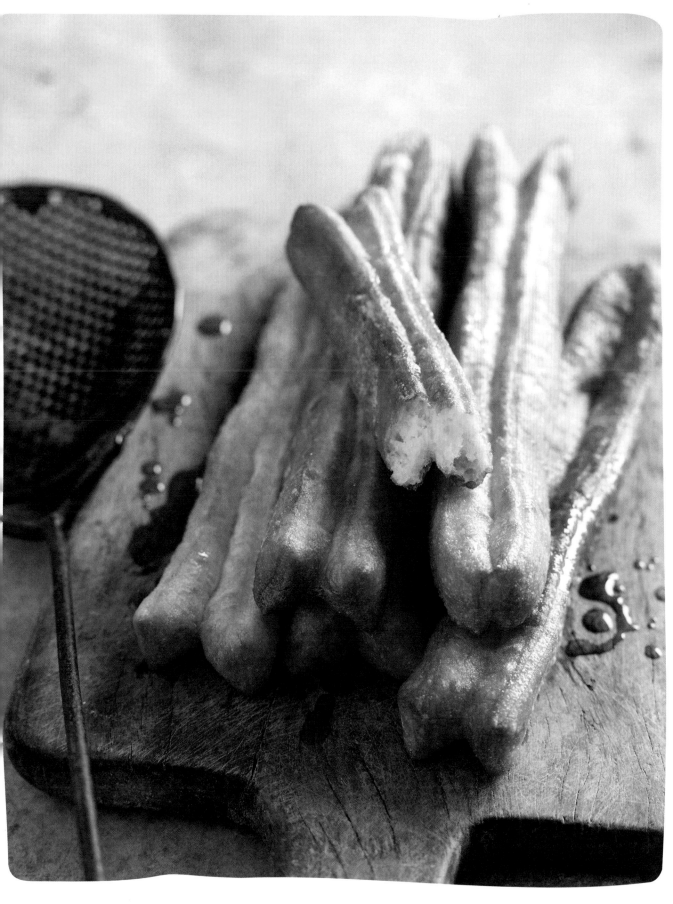

 PINK-ICED CANADIAN DONUTS

Originating in the city of Thunder Bay, Canada, these sweet cinnamon scroll donuts are topped with icing made from fresh raspberries and sometimes strawberries.

PERSIANS
2 tablespoons lukewarm water, plus 125 ml (4 fl oz/½ cup) extra
2 teaspoons dried yeast
55 g (2 oz/¼ cup) caster (superfine) sugar
¼ teaspoon fine sea salt
1 teaspoon ground cinnamon
2 teaspoons vanilla essence
1 egg, at room temperature, lightly whisked
30 g (1 oz) unsalted butter, melted, at room temperature
375 g (13 oz/2½ cups) plain (all-purpose) flour, plus extra for dusting
Vegetable, canola or rice bran oil, for deep-frying

FOR DUSTING
55 g (2 oz/¼ cup, firmly packed) brown sugar
2 teaspoons ground cinnamon

RASPBERRY ICING
50 g (1¾ oz) raspberries
125 g (4½ oz/1 cup) icing (confectioners') sugar

WHISK the 2 tablespoons of lukewarm water with the yeast in a small, heatproof jug. Add the caster sugar and whisk until well combined. Allow to stand in a warm spot for 10–15 minutes, or until frothy.

ADD the salt, cinnamon, vanilla essence, egg, butter, flour, the remaining 125 ml of water and the yeast mixture to the bowl of a standmixer. Attach the dough hook and mix together on a medium speed until well combined, then mix for 5 minutes more, or until the dough is smooth and elastic (the dough will feel slightly sticky).

USING very lightly floured hands, scrape the dough into a lightly oiled bowl. Cover with a piece of baking paper, then a tea towel (dish towel) and set aside to rest in a warm, draught-free spot for 1–1½ hours, or until the dough has doubled in size.

LIGHTLY flour a clean surface and rolling pin and roll the dough into a rectangle about 42 x 30 cm (17 x 12 inches). Combine the brown sugar and cinnamon for dusting, then sprinkle it evenly over the surface of the dough. Roll the dough up tightly from the long side to form one long log. Trim the ends so that the log is about 40 cm (16 inches) in length.

LINE two baking trays with baking paper. Cut the log into 12 equal pieces, then transfer to the lined baking trays, cut-side facing up. Lightly flatten each piece of dough with the palm of your hand to a 1.5 cm (⅝ inch) thick round. Cover the trays with tea towels and allow to rest for 1 hour at room temperature in a warm spot or until doubled in size.

HEAT the oil in a deep, heavy-based saucepan over a medium–high heat until it reaches 180°C (350°F). Deep-fry the donuts in batches, turning occasionally, for 2–3 minutes each, or until puffed, golden and cooked through. Transfer to paper towels to drain briefly, then transfer to a wire rack set over a baking tray.

MASH the raspberries for the icing with a fork in a small bowl, then push them through a fine sieve and discard any seeds left behind. Whisk the raspberry purée and icing sugar together until well combined and smooth.

DRIZZLE the raspberry icing over the warm donuts, then allow to set before serving.

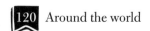

Donut tower cake

Halloween donuts

Strawberry heart donuts

Neapolitan ice-cream donut sandwiches

Champagne-cream donut bites

Christmas donuts

Chocolate sparkle donuts

CHAPTER 7

SHOW-STOPPERS AND JAW-DROPPERS

DONUT TOWER CAKE

This is the perfect celebratory cake for all ages, and will really wow your guests. Get everyone involved in the decorating to make it truly unique.

CAKE DONUTS
80 g (2¾ oz) unsalted butter, at room temperature
110 g (3¾ oz/½ cup) caster (superfine) sugar
1 egg, at room temperature
1 egg yolk, at room temperature
1 teaspoon vanilla essence
250 ml (9 fl oz/1 cup) milk
55 g (2oz/½ cup) cocoa powder
500 g (1 lb 2 oz/3⅓ cups) self-raising flour, plus extra for dusting
A good pinch of fine sea salt
Vegetable, canola or rice bran oil, for deep-frying

TO DECORATE
110 g (3¾ oz/½ cup) caster (superfine) sugar
Hundreds and thousands
White sprinkles

RASPBERRY CREAM CHEESE ICING
40 g (1½ oz) unsalted butter, at room temperature
125 g (4½ oz) cream cheese, at room temperature
50 g (1¾ oz) raspberries
160 g (5¾ oz/1⅓ cups) icing (confectioners') sugar, plus extra for dusting

CREAM the butter and sugar together in a large standmixer for 3 minutes, or until pale and fluffy. Add the egg, egg yolk, vanilla essence and milk and mix until just combined.

SIFT the cocoa, flour and salt over the mixture in the bowl. Mix until just combined, but do not overmix or the dough will become tough.

LIGHTLY flour a clean surface, turn the dough out onto it and, using lightly floured hands, gently bring it together. Knead gently for a few seconds until the dough becomes smooth. Using a floured rolling pin, gently roll the dough out to a 1 cm (½ inch) thickness. Using a floured 8 cm (3¼ inch) round cookie cutter, cut out rounds from the dough, making sure you cut them as close together as possible. Re-roll any off-cuts and cut out more rounds until you have 12 in total. Use a floured 3 cm (1¼ inch) round cookie cutter to cut out holes from the centre of each larger circle.

PUT the caster sugar for coating in a deep, heatproof bowl.

HEAT the oil in a deep, heavy-based saucepan over a medium–high heat until it reaches 180°C (350°F). Deep-fry the donuts in batches, turning occasionally, for 2–3 minutes each, or until puffed, golden and cooked through. Transfer to paper towels to drain briefly then, while still hot, roll only the edges of the donuts in sugar. Allow to cool.

BEAT the butter for the icing for 3 minutes, or until pale and creamy. Add the remaining icing ingredients and beat until well combined and smooth.

SPOON the icing over the tops of the cooled donuts. Stack the donuts in a tower on a cake stand. Decorate with the hundreds and thousands and white sprinkles, then dust with extra icing sugar before serving.

HALLOWEEN DONUTS

Impress your trick-or-treaters with these deliciously spooky pumpkin-pie donuts.

CAKE DONUTS

80 g (2¾ oz) unsalted butter, at room temperature
110 g (3¾ oz/½ cup) caster (superfine) sugar
1 egg, at room temperature
1 egg yolk, at room temperature
1 teaspoon vanilla essence
½ teaspoon ground mixed spice
200 g (7 oz/¾ cup) cooked and mashed pumpkin
80 ml (2½ fl oz/⅓ cup) milk
550 g (1 lb 4 oz/3⅔ cups) self-raising flour, plus extra for dusting
A good pinch of fine sea salt
Vegetable, canola or rice bran oil, for deep-frying

VANILLA NUTMEG GLAZE

185 g (6½ oz/1½ cups) icing (confectioners') sugar
2 teaspoons vanilla bean paste
A good pinch of freshly grated nutmeg

TO SERVE

60 g (2¼ oz/1½ cups) caramel popcorn, broken into pieces
Black writing icing

CREAM the butter and sugar together in a large standmixer for 3 minutes, or until pale and fluffy. Add the egg, egg yolk, vanilla essence, mixed spice, pumpkin and milk and mix until just combined.

SIFT the flour and salt over the mixture in the bowl. Mix until just combined, but do not overmix or the dough will become tough.

LIGHTLY flour a clean surface, turn the dough out onto it and, using lightly floured hands, gently bring it together. Knead gently for a few seconds until the dough becomes smooth. Using a floured rolling pin, gently roll the dough out to a 1 cm (½ inch) thickness. Using a floured 8 cm (3¼ inch) round cookie cutter, cut out rounds from the dough, making sure you cut them as close together as possible. Re-roll any off-cuts and cut out more rounds until you have 12 in total. Use a floured 3 cm (1¼ inch) round cookie cutter to cut out holes from the centre of each larger circle.

HEAT the oil in a deep, heavy-based saucepan over a medium–high heat until it reaches 180°C (350°F). Deep-fry the donuts in batches for 2–3 minutes each, turning occasionally, or until puffed, golden and cooked through. Transfer to paper towels to drain briefly, then allow to cool.

WHISK all the ingredients for the glaze together in a bowl with 2 tablespoons of water until well combined and smooth.

DIP the cooled donuts, one at a time, into the glaze. Transfer to a wire rack set over a baking tray. Sprinkle the tops with caramel popcorn, then decorate with black writing icing and allow to set before serving.

STRAWBERRY HEART DONUTS

Spoil your true love with these little bites of strawberry sweetness. So much better than a bunch of roses.

CAKE DONUTS

80 g (2¾ oz) unsalted butter, at room temperature
110 g (3¾ oz/½ cup) caster (superfine) sugar
1 egg, at room temperature
1 egg yolk, at room temperature
1 teaspoon vanilla essence
185 ml (6 fl oz/¾ cup) milk
500 g (1 lb 2 oz/3⅓ cups) self-raising flour, plus extra for dusting
A good pinch of fine sea salt
20 g (¾ oz/1½ cups) freeze-dried strawberries
Vegetable, canola or rice bran oil, for deep-frying

STRAWBERRY ICING

125 g (4½ oz/1 cup) icing (confectioners') sugar, plus extra for dusting
2 teaspoons imitation strawberry essence
1 tablespoon milk
6 drops of pink food colouring

CREAM the butter and sugar together in a large standmixer for 3 minutes, or until pale and fluffy. Add the egg, egg yolk, vanilla essence and milk and mix until just combined.

SIFT the flour and salt over the mixture in the bowl. Add half of the freeze-dried strawberries and mix until just combined, but do not overmix or the dough will become tough.

LIGHTLY flour a clean surface, turn the dough out onto it and, using lightly floured hands, gently bring it together. Knead gently for a few seconds until the dough becomes smooth. Using a floured rolling pin, gently roll the dough out to a 1 cm (½ inch) thickness. Using a floured 6 cm (2½ inch) heart-shaped cookie cutter, cut out hearts from the dough, making sure you cut them as close together as possible. Re-roll any off-cuts and cut out more hearts until you have 18 in total.

HEAT the oil in a deep, heavy-based saucepan over a medium–high heat until it reaches 180°C (350°F). Deep-fry the donuts in batches, turning occasionally, for 2–3 minutes each, or until puffed, golden and cooked through. Transfer to paper towels to drain briefly, then allow to cool.

WHISK all the ingredients for the strawberry icing together in a bowl until well combined and smooth.

TRANSFER the donuts to a wire rack set over a baking tray. Drizzle the icing over the cooled donuts. Sprinkle the tops with the remaining freeze-dried strawberries, then allow to set before dusting with extra icing sugar and serving.

NEAPOLITAN ICE-CREAM DONUT SANDWICHES

A great summer outdoor treat.

CAKE DONUTS
80 g (2¾ oz) unsalted butter,
    at room temperature
110 g (3¾ oz/½ cup) caster
    (superfine) sugar
1 egg, at room temperature
1 egg yolk, at room temperature
1 teaspoon vanilla essence
185 ml (6 fl oz/¾ cup) milk
500 g (1 lb 2 oz/3⅓ cups)
    self-raising flour, plus
    extra for dusting
A good pinch of fine sea salt
Vegetable, canola or rice bran
    oil, for deep-frying

VANILLA ICING
120 g (4¼ oz/¾ cup) icing
    (confectioners') sugar
1 teaspoon vanilla essence
1 tablespoon boiling water

STRAWBERRY ICING
120 g (4¼ oz/¾ cup) icing
    (confectioners') sugar
1 teaspoon imitation
    strawberry essence
8 drops of red food colouring
1 tablespoon boiling water

CHOCOLATE ICING
80 g (2¾ oz/½ cup) icing
    (confectioners') sugar
2 tablespoons cocoa powder
2 tablespoons boiling water

TO SERVE
Hundreds and thousands
12 scoops Neapolitan ice cream

CREAM the butter and sugar together in a large standmixer for 3 minutes, or until pale and fluffy. Add the egg, egg yolk, vanilla essence and milk and mix until just combined.

SIFT the flour and salt over the mixture in the bowl. Mix until just combined, but do not overmix or the dough will become tough.

LIGHTLY flour a clean surface, turn the dough out onto it and, using lightly floured hands, gently bring it together. Knead gently for a few seconds until the dough becomes smooth. Using a floured rolling pin, gently roll the dough out to a 1 cm (½ inch) thickness. Using a floured 8 cm (3¼ inch) round cookie cutter, cut out rounds from the dough, making sure you cut them as close together as possible. Re-roll any off-cuts and cut out more rounds until you have 12 in total.

HEAT the oil in a deep, heavy-based saucepan over a medium–high heat until it reaches 180°C (350°F). Deep-fry the donuts in batches, turning occasionally, for 2–3 minutes each, or until puffed, golden and cooked through. Transfer to paper towels to drain briefly, then allow to cool completely.

WHISK together the ingredients for each icing in separate bowls until well combined and smooth.

SPOON the icing over the donuts so you have four iced with vanilla, four with strawberry and four with chocolate. Transfer the donuts to a wire rack set over a baking tray and sprinkle their tops with hundreds and thousands. Allow to set.

WHEN you're ready to serve, carefully cut each donut in half and place a scoop of ice cream at the centre. Replace the top and serve immediately.

CHAMPAGNE-CREAM DONUT BITES

These exquisite bites will make any celebration extra special.

YEAST DONUTS

60 ml (2 fl oz/¼ cup) lukewarm water
3½ teaspoons dried yeast
450 g (1 lb/3 cups) plain (all-purpose) flour, plus extra for dusting
55 g (2 oz/¼ cup) caster (superfine) sugar
½ teaspoon fine sea salt
1 egg, at room temperature, lightly whisked
30 g (1 oz) unsalted butter, melted, at room temperature
185 ml (6 fl oz/¾ cup) Champagne
Vegetable, canola or rice bran oil, for deep-frying
375 ml (13 fl oz/1½ cups) crème anglaise or thick vanilla-bean custard

TO COAT

220 g (7¾ oz/1 cup) sugar
2 teaspoons edible sliver glitter, plus extra, to serve

ROYAL ICING

1 egg white, at room temperature
185 g (6½ oz/1½ cups) icing (confectioners') sugar
1 teaspoon lemon juice

WHISK the water and yeast together in a small, heatproof jug. Add 1 teaspoon of the flour and 1 teaspoon of the sugar and whisk until well combined. Leave to stand at room temperature in a warm spot for 10–15 minutes, or until frothy.

PLACE the remaining flour, remaining sugar and the salt in the bowl of a standmixer. Attach the dough hook and mix together on a medium speed until well combined.

WITH the motor running, slowly add the egg, melted butter, Champagne and then the yeast mixture. Mix for 8 minutes, or until the dough is smooth and elastic (the dough should feel slightly sticky).

USING very lightly floured hands, scrape the dough into a lightly oiled bowl. Cover with a piece of baking paper, then a tea towel (dish towel). Set aside to rest at room temperature in a warm, draught-free spot for 1–1½ hours, or until the dough has doubled in size.

LINE two large baking trays with baking paper. Generously flour a work surface and gently tip the dough out onto it. Using a floured rolling pin, gently roll the dough out to a 1 cm (½ inch) thickness. Using a floured 6 cm (2½ inch) round cookie cutter, cut out 18 rounds from the dough, making sure you cut them as close together as possible. Carefully transfer the donuts to the prepared trays, spreading them out in a single layer. Cover with tea towels and leave to rest for 40 minutes at room temperature or until doubled in size.

COMBINE the sugar and edible silver glitter in a deep, heatproof bowl.

HEAT the oil in a deep, heavy-based saucepan over a medium–high heat until it reaches 180°C (350°F). Deep-fry the donuts in batches, turning occasionally, for 2–3 minutes each, or until puffed, golden and cooked through. Transfer to paper towels to drain briefly then, while still hot, toss in the silver sugar to coat. Allow to cool.

SPOON the crème anglaise into a piping bag fitted with a 5 mm (¼ inch) round nozzle. Pipe this into the donut centres.

BEAT the egg white for the royal icing until frothy, then add the icing sugar, a tablespoon at a time, beating until the mixture is thick and glossy. Beat in the juice until combined. Spoon the icing into a piping bag fitted with a 1 cm (½ inch) round nozzle and pipe a small round on top of each donut. Sprinkle with the extra silver glitter and serve.

CHRISTMAS DONUTS

Not only do these donuts look the part, but every bite is full of traditional Christmas flavour.

CAKE DONUTS
80 g (2¾ oz) unsalted butter, at room temperature
110 g (3¾ oz/½ cup) caster (superfine) sugar
1 egg, at room temperature
1 egg yolk, at room temperature
1 teaspoon vanilla essence
185 ml (6 fl oz/¾ cup) milk
235 g (8½ oz/¾ cup) fruit mince
550 g (1 lb 4 oz/3⅔ cups) self-raising flour, plus extra for dusting
A good pinch of fine sea salt
Vegetable, canola or rice bran oil, for deep-frying

TO COAT
220 g (7¾ oz/1 cup) sugar
2 teaspoons ground cinnamon

BRANDY ICING
125 g (4½ oz/1 cup) icing (confectioners') sugar
2 teaspoons imitation brandy essence
3 teaspoons boiling water

TO SERVE
Red and green sprinkles

CREAM the butter and sugar together in a large standmixer for 3 minutes, or until pale and fluffy. Add the egg, egg yolk, vanilla essence, milk and fruit mince and mix until just combined.

SIFT the flour and salt over the mixture in the bowl. Mix until just combined, but do not overmix or the dough will become tough.

LIGHTLY flour a clean surface, turn the dough out onto it and, using lightly floured hands, gently bring it together. Knead gently for a few seconds until the dough becomes smooth. Using a floured rolling pin, gently roll the dough out to a 1 cm (½ inch) thickness. Using a floured 8 cm (3¼ inch) round cookie cutter, cut out rounds from the dough, making sure you cut them as close together as possible. Re-roll any off-cuts and cut out more rounds until you have 12 in total. Use a floured 3 cm (1¼ inch) round cookie cutter to cut out holes from the centre of each larger circle.

COMBINE the sugar and cinnamon, for coating the donuts, in a deep, heatproof bowl.

HEAT the oil in a deep, heavy-based saucepan over a medium–high heat until it reaches 180°C (350°F). Deep-fry the donuts in batches, turning occasionally, for 2–3 minutes each, or until puffed, golden and cooked through. Transfer to paper towels to drain briefly then, while still hot, roll in the cinnamon sugar to coat on all sides. Allow to cool.

WHISK all the ingredients for the brandy icing together until well combined and smooth.

DRIZZLE the icing over the donuts. Transfer to a wire rack set over a baking tray, then top with the sprinkles. Allow to set before serving.

CHOCOLATE SPARKLE DONUTS

Give any special occasion all the glitz and glamour it deserves with these stand-out treats, using touches of edible gold to keep the night sparkly.

YEAST DONUTS

250 ml (9 fl oz/1 cup) lukewarm milk
3½ teaspoons dried yeast
450 g (1 lb/3 cups) plain (all-purpose) flour, plus extra for dusting
55 g (2 oz/¼ cup) caster (superfine) sugar
½ teaspoon fine sea salt
1 egg, at room temperature, lightly whisked
30 g (1 oz) unsalted butter, melted, at room temperature
Vegetable, canola or rice bran oil, for deep-frying

CHOCOLATE GANACHE

200 g (7 oz) dark chocolate, chopped
60 ml (2 fl oz/¼ cup) thin (pouring) cream

TO SERVE

375 ml (13 fl oz/1½ cups) extra thick chocolate custard
Edible gold glitter, mini stars and gold cachous

WHISK the milk and yeast together in a small, heatproof jug. Add 1 teaspoon of the flour and 1 teaspoon of the sugar and whisk until well combined. Allow to stand at room temperature in a warm spot for 10–15 minutes or until frothy.

PLACE the remaining flour, remaining sugar and the salt in the bowl of a standmixer. Attach the dough hook and mix together on a medium speed until well combined.

WITH the motor running, slowly add the egg, melted butter and the yeast mixture. Mix for 8 minutes, or until the dough is smooth and elastic (the dough should feel slightly sticky).

USING very lightly floured hands, scrape the dough into a lightly oiled bowl. Cover with a piece of baking paper, then a tea towel (dish towel). Set aside to rest at room temperature in a warm, draught-free spot for 1–1½ hours, or until the dough has doubled in size.

LINE two large baking trays with baking paper. Generously flour a work surface and gently tip the dough out onto it. Using a floured rolling pin, gently roll the dough out to a 1 cm (½ inch) thickness. Using a floured 8 cm (3¼ inch) round cookie cutter, cut out 10 rounds from the dough, making sure you cut them as close together as possible. Use a floured 3 cm (1¼ inch) round cookie cutter to cut out holes from the centre of each larger circle. Carefully transfer to the prepared trays, spreading them out in a single layer. Cover with tea towels and rest for 40 minutes at room temperature or until doubled in size.

HEAT the oil in a deep, heavy-based saucepan over a medium–high heat until it reaches 180°C (350°F). Deep-fry the donuts in batches, turning occasionally, for 2–3 minutes each, or until puffed, golden and cooked through. Transfer to paper towels to drain. Cool, then cut in half.

PLACE all the ingredients for the chocolate ganache in a heatproof bowl set over a simmering saucepan of water, making sure the base of the bowl doesn't touch the water. Stir gently until the mixture melts and is smooth. Remove the bowl from the heat, and leave to cool to room temperature, stirring occasionally, for 1 hour, or until set softly to a spreadable consistency.

SPOON the chocolate custard over one cut-side of each donut, then replace the donut tops. Spread the tops with ganache, then sprinkle with gold glitter, stars and cachous and serve.

Index

Page numbers in italics refer to photographs.

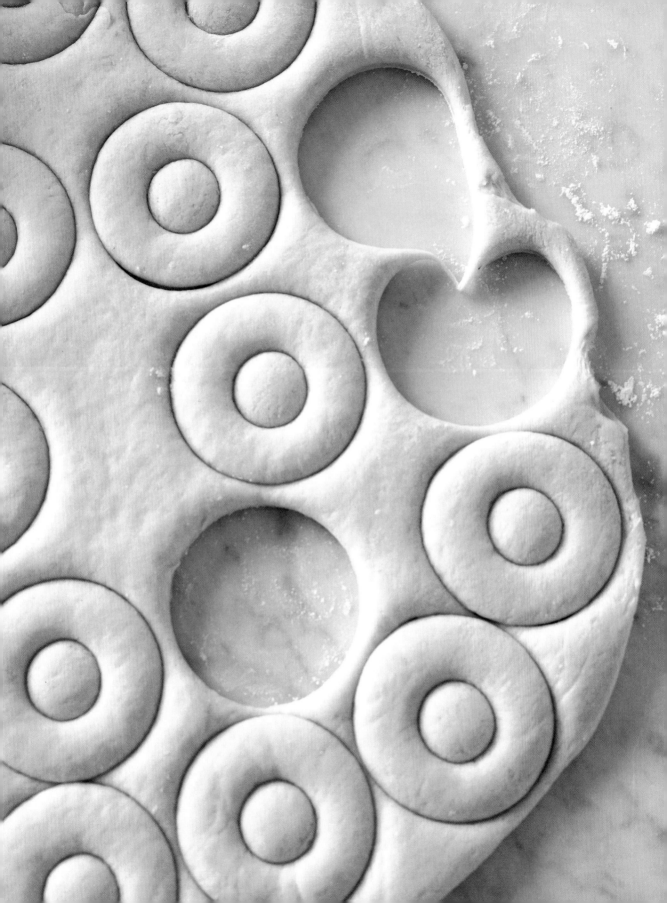

Published in 2014 by Murdoch Books, an imprint of Allen & Unwin

Murdoch Books Australia
83 Alexander Street
Crows Nest NSW 2065
Phone: +61 (0) 2 8425 0100
Fax: +61 (0) 2 9906 2218
www.murdochbooks.com.au
info@murdochbooks.com.au

Murdoch Books UK
Erico House, 6th Floor
93–99 Upper Richmond Road
Putney, London SW15 2TG
Phone: +44 (0) 20 8785 5995
www.murdochbooks.co.uk
info@murdochbooks.co.uk

For Corporate Orders & Custom Publishing contact
Noel Hammond, National Business Development Manager, Murdoch Books Australia

Publisher: Jane Morrow
Editorial Manager: Virginia Birch
Design Manager: Hugh Ford
Recipe Developer and Home Economist: Tracey Meharg
Editor: Katie Bosher
Design: Dan Peterson & Jacqui Porter, Northwood Green
Photographer: Rob Palmer
Stylist: Michelle Noerianto
Assistant Home Economist: Theressa Klein
Production Manager: Mary Bjelobrk

A cataloguing-in-publication entry is available from the catalogue of the National Library
of Australia at www.nla.gov.au.

ISBN 978 1 74336 307 2 Australia
ISBN 978 1 74336 323 2 UK

A catalogue record for this book is available from the British Library.

Colour reproduction by Splitting Image Colour Studio Pty Ltd, Clayton, Victoria
Printed by 1010 Printing International Limited, China

IMPORTANT: Those who might be at risk from the effects of salmonella poisoning (the elderly,
pregnant women, young children and those suffering from immune deficiency diseases) should
consult their doctor with any concerns about eating raw eggs.

OVEN GUIDE: You may find cooking times vary depending on the oven you are using. For fan-forced
ovens, as a general rule, set the oven temperature to 20°C (35°F) lower than indicated in the recipe.

MEASURES GUIDE: We have used 20 ml (4 teaspoon) tablespoon measures. If you are using a
15 ml (3 teaspoon) tablespoon add an extra teaspoon of the ingredient for each tablespoon specified.